BLAZING
BARBECUE

BLAZING BARBECUE

101 RECIPES FOR BRILLIANT BARBECUES

MARKS &
SPENCER

Marks and Spencer p.l.c.
PO Box 3339
Chester CH99 9QS

shop online
www.marksandspencer.com

ISBN: 978-1-84960-601-1

Printed in China

Cover photography by Mike Cooper
Food styling by Lincoln Jefferson
Introduction and new recipes by Christine McFadden

The views expressed in this book are those of the author but they are general views only and readers are urged to consult a relevant and qualified specialist for individual advice in particular situations. Marks and Spencer p.l.c. and Exclusive Editions Limited hereby exclude all liability to the extent permitted by law for any errors or omissions in this book and for any loss, damage or expense (whether direct or indirect) suffered by a third party relying on any information contained in this book.

Notes for the Reader
This book uses both metric and imperial measurements. Follow the same units of measurement throughout; do not mix metric and imperial. All spoon measurements are level: teaspoons are assumed to be 5 ml, and tablespoons are assumed to be 15 ml. Unless otherwise stated, milk is assumed to be full fat, eggs and individual vegetables are medium, and pepper is freshly ground black pepper.

The times given are an approximate guide only. Preparation times differ according to the techniques used by different people and the cooking times may also vary from those given. Optional ingredients, variations or serving suggestions have not been included in the calculations.

Recipes using raw or very lightly cooked eggs should be avoided by infants, the elderly, pregnant women, convalescents and anyone suffering from an illness. Pregnant and breastfeeding women are advised to avoid eating peanuts and peanut products. Sufferers from nut allergies should be aware that some of the ready-made ingredients used in the recipes in this book may contain nuts. Always check the packaging before use.

Vegetarians should be aware that some of the ingredients and ready-made items used in the recipes in this book may contain animal products which make them unsuitable for a vegetarian diet. Always check the packaging and seek out vegetarian alternatives where needed.

Picture Acknowledgements

The publisher would like to thank the following for permission to reproduce copyright material:

Getty Images, pages: 2, 6–7 14–15, 38–39, 48–49, 56–57, 82–83, 90–91, 122–123, 140–141, 150–151, 182–183, 206–207, 215, 216–217, 222–223

Contents

INTRODUCTION

There is nothing quite like barbecuing for bringing out the best in food – it simply looks better, smells better and tastes better. The smoke and the charring add a depth of flavour that's hard to beat, and the heart-warming sight of glowing coals takes us back to our campfire origins. Now that many of us choose to eat in rather than out, barbecuing has become the popular way to cook and get together with friends and family. From everyday suppers to celebration dinners, you can cook great barbecue food at almost any time of year, including Christmas.

GETTING STARTED
Choosing a barbecue
Modern barbecues come in a tempting variety of shapes, sizes, styles and prices, from disposable picnic barbecues, to no-frills portable models, and those with all the latest bells and whistles. There are also ingenious accessories, such as rib racks, vegetable baskets, poultry roasters and pizza stones, which make it possible to cook an inspiring range of foods, turning the average barbecue into a much more stylish affair.

When choosing a barbecue, think about how many people you are likely to cook for. If the barbecue is too small, the grill will be crowded and the food won't cook properly. If it is too big, you will waste fuel. As a rule of thumb, you need a grilling area of 30 x 30 cm/12 x 12 inches, or 35 cm/ 14 inches in diameter for four to six people.

Fuel
Charcoal is by far the best fuel for that essential smoky chargrilled flavour. Use mineral or hardwood briquettes rather than lump-wood charcoal. Briquettes burn for longer and more evenly, and they produce less ash to blow around and stick to the food.

Useful equipment
* Chimney starter: a large hollow metal cylinder with a wooden handle and a wire mesh partition near the base.
* Long-handled stiff wire brush for cleaning the grill grate.
* Small garden rake or long-handled tongs for arranging coals.
* Long-handled utensils: tongs, spatulas and a basting brush.
* Hinged square or rectangular wire racks for holding and turning fragile food.

* Hinged shaped wire holders for kebabs, whole fish, sardines and sausages.
* Metal and bamboo skewers.
* Foil drip trays for cooking with indirect heat (see page 8).
* Instant-read thermometer for checking the internal temperature of meat and poultry.
* Small pointed knife for checking doneness of small items.
* Long thick oven mitts.
* Water spray bottle for damping down flare-ups.
* Large torch or other lighting for checking food after dark. This is particularly important for fish and poultry.

Lighting the barbecue
Don't be tempted to douse the charcoal with lighter fuel or paraffin and toss in a lit match. Not only could this cause an explosion, the food will be tainted with the unpleasant taste of the fuel. Instant-lighting firelighters are also to be avoided as they taint the flavour.

Self-lighting charcoal is easily available, but it is impregnated with lighter fuel and even if 'odourless', may still give off an unwelcome flavour. It's far better to use a chimney starter (see Useful Equipment, left), or good old-fashioned newspaper and kindling.

To light the chimney starter, place it in the base of the barbecue or on a fireproof slab. Stuff crumpled newspaper under the wire partition, and fill the top part with charcoal briquettes. Light the paper with a gas lighter or long match. Keep stuffing twisted pieces of newspaper through the ventilation holes until you are sure the charcoal has ignited. The coals will be ready in 20–25 minutes when they are all glowing orange. Tip them into the barbecue and rake them into your chosen arrangement (see Temperature Control, page 8). If the food will take more than one hour to cook, light a second chimney for replenishing the fire.

To light the barbecue with newspaper and kindling, pile small pieces of kindling, or sap-saturated wooden starter sticks, on top of some crumpled newspaper. Ignite the newspaper, and once the kindling starts to burn, mound the briquettes in an igloo shape on top. Once the coals are glowing orange, rake them into your chosen arrangement (see Arranging the Coals, page 8). To replenish the fire with unlit charcoal, rake the remaining embers into a pile and place fresh briquettes on top. Once glowing orange, spread out the coals as before.

Cleaning the grill grate

It's important to start off with a clean grill grate. A dirty grate is unhygienic, it makes the food stick, and adds unwelcome flavours.

Cleaning takes only a minute or two, and doesn't involve soap, water, special cleaners or messy scrubbing in a sink. Just place the grate in position over lit coals, and once hot, scrub it with a dry stiff wire brush to remove debris. It's a good idea to give the grate another scrub between batches of food, especially fish and seafood, and a final scrub once you have finished cooking.

Oiling the grill grate

Once the grate is clean, it should be oiled to prevent food sticking. The easiest way is to soak a wad of paper towel with vegetable oil. Grasp the wad with long-handled tongs and rub firmly over the bars of the grate.

An oil-spray is another option, but make sure you remove the grate and hold it well away from the fire while you spray. Never use an oil-spray with the grate in position – the droplets can easily catch fire and cause dangerous flare-up.

Barbecue safety

- Never leave a lit barbecue unattended.
- Don't allow small children or pets near the barbecue.
- Don't leave bags of charcoal, barbecue lids or other equipment on the ground where people might trip over them.
- Keep a water-spray handy for dealing with flare-ups.
- Protect yourself from the heat with long barbecue mitts and long-handled tools.
- When you have finished cooking, push the coals away from the centre to speed up cooling. Remember that embers that look grey may still be hot.
- Don't move the barbecue until the fire is out and the coals are cold.

COOKING ON THE BARBECUE

Though it looks simple, successful grilling on a charcoal barbecue depends on temperature and timing, as well as good-quality ingredients. If you're new to barbecuing, start by trying a few simple recipes first, and then you can expand your repertoire. Once you have mastered the basics, you'll be able to rustle up scrumptious, perfectly barbecued food with confidence – from simple kebabs and burgers to whole roast joints of meat, inspiring vegetarian dishes and delicious desserts.

SPECIAL OCCASIONS

Barbecues are perfect for celebrating special occasions, and often preferable to a formal meal in a restaurant. Modern equipment means that the food can be inspirational, yet still easy to prepare and fun to cook. Try the magnificent Herb-crusted Beef Fillet (page 18), or create a Caribbean theme with Jamaican Jerk Pork Fillet (page 43), or push the boat out and serve lobster (page 129). Non-meat eaters can enjoy sumptuous vegetable dishes such as Portobello Ciabatta Burgers (page 139) or a colourful Italian Vegetable Platter (page 176). Mouth-watering fruit desserts can be given the barbecue treatment too, and will taste even better that way.

If you are catering for a large number of guests, it's a good idea to have two or three barbecues on the go – one for quick direct grilling, another for slow-cooked items and a third for vegetarian dishes. With judicious timing, the food can be served when you want it, without fear of the fire losing heat.

Special lighting adds to the sense of occasion. Solar lights or neon glow sticks positioned along the driveway create a welcoming effect after dark. Strings of sparkling stars festooned in trees and over parasols transform your garden into a night-time wonderland. Tea lights on tables create a warm, romantic glow.

Don't let a sudden downpour ruin the occasion. An open-sided gazebo provides shelter with enough ventilation for cooking, and a kettle barbecue with a lid means you can carry on cooking regardless. Your guests may have to move indoors, but the food will still have that fabulous chargrilled flavour.

GRILLING TECHNIQUES

There are several ways of grilling on the barbecue, each one designed to bring out the best in the food according to its size, thickness and texture.

Direct grilling

As the name suggests, the food is cooked on the grill grate directly over a layer of very hot coals. Direct grilling is perfect for small or thin items of food such as kebabs, fish fillets, steaks and burgers that cook quickly.

Indirect grilling

With indirect grilling, the coals are arranged on opposite sides of the barbecue with a foil drip tray in the middle. The food is cooked on the grill grate in the cooler central area over the drip tray, and usually covered with a lid. Indirect grilling is best for food that needs longer cooking over medium–hot coals, such as joints of meat, whole poultry or large fish (see Temperature Control, opposite).

Grilling in parcels

The food is loosely wrapped in well-sealed foil, or sturdy fibrous leaves such as vine or banana leaves, or sweetcorn husks. The parcels are cooked either on the grill grate or nestling in the embers. The food cooks in its own steam so it remains moist and flavoursome. Chunky root vegetables are particularly good cooked this way (see Beetroot Parcels, page 169), as are whole fish (see Keralan Spiced Fish, page 114).

TEMPERATURE CONTROL

The trick to successful grilling is understanding how to control the cooking temperature. This depends on the type and amount of charcoal you are using, the way it is arranged on the grill, and the length of time it has been burning. There are also other variables to contend with, such as the temperature outside, altitude and wind. Remember that coals can lose as much as 25 per cent of their heat after one hour unless they are replenished.

Assessing the heat

Hold the flat of your hand about 10 cm/4 inches above the fire. Count the number of seconds before the intensity of the heat forces you to remove your hand. For accuracy, use a watch with a second hand; alternatively, insert a three- or four-syllable word between each count, as in 'one barbecue, two barbecue, three barbecue'.

Heat of coals	Temperature	Seconds
Hot	230°–290°C/450°–550°F	2–3
Medium-hot	200°C/400°F	4–5
Medium	170°–180°C/325°–350°F	6–8
Medium-low	150°C/300°F	9–10
Low	110°–120°C/225°–250°F	11–14

Arranging the coals

Once lit and glowing orange, the coals can be arranged in different ways to create very hot, medium–hot and cooler areas.

- For simple direct grilling, rake the coals into a single layer. It's a good idea to leave a small coal-free area at the edge for parking food if it starts to burn.
- To create a dual-heat fire for food that needs searing at high heat then cooking at a lower temperature, rake some of the coals into a two-layer heap on one side, leaving a cooler single layer on the other side.
- To create a triple-heat fire, repeat the dual-heat arrangement as above, leaving the single layer of coals in the middle, and a coal-free area to one side for keeping cooked food warm.

Other methods of temperature control

Depending on the type of barbecue:

- Adjust the vents in the sides or bottom of the barbecue. More oxygen makes the coals burn hotter; less will cool them down.
- Raise or lower the grill grate.
- Cover the food with a lid with open vents.

Cooking sequence

Start off by cooking food that can be served at room temperature, or food that needs to be left to stand before carving, such as joints of meat, large whole fish or poultry. These should be left for at least 10 minutes to allow the juices to flow back evenly through the food.

Next, cook smaller, quickly cooked items such as seafood, burgers and kebabs, for serving immediately when people are ready to eat. Heat burger buns and pitta bread at the same time.

Cook desserts while you are eating the rest of the meal, and the fire has started to cool down.

COOK'S TIPS
Getting organized

Before you start to cook, assemble essentials on a work table close to the barbecue – seasonings, sauces, oils, marinades, herbs and lemons. Then you won't have to rush back to the kitchen in the middle of cooking.

Temperature of uncooked food

Don't cook meat and poultry directly from the refrigerator – it takes longer to cook, and won't brown evenly. Take it out of the refrigerator at least 30 minutes before cooking. Keep it covered while it loses its chill.

Successful searing

Resist the urge to inspect the underside of the food too soon. If you do so, it won't form a crust and the food will stick to the grill grate. Depending on the type of food, it usually takes at least 3–4 minutes for the lower surface to brown.

Keeping meat juicy

Resist the temptation to poke and prod at steaks and burgers. This is a natural habit, but all it does is make holes, causing succulent juices to drain away and the food to become dry.

Tasty gravy

When cooking by the indirect method, pour some liquid – either stock or water – into the drip tray below the food. Add herbs and slivers of vegetables if you like. Juices will trickle from the meat or poultry above, combining with the liquid to make tasty gravy.

Protecting food from flies and wasps

- Cover bulky items of food with an oval wire-mesh cover or nylon food umbrella.
- Use clingfilm or foil to cover bowls and shallow dishes.
- To trap wasps, punch a hole in the metal lid of an old screw-top jar. Pour some watered-down jam into the bottom of the jar and the wasps will crawl in.

FOOD SAFETY

- Allow frozen food to thaw completely in the refrigerator and reach room temperature before barbecuing.
- Keep raw meat, poultry or fish on a plate or plastic tray. Do not place it directly on the work surface.
- Wash your hands thoroughly after handling raw meat, poultry or fish. Do not simply wipe them on a towel or apron.
- Use one set of tools to transfer raw food to the barbecue, and another set for handling cooked food. Never touch cooked meat or poultry with tools that have been in contact with raw meat or poultry.
- Don't brush cooked food with marinade that has been in contact with raw meat, poultry or fish. If you want to use left-over marinade as a sauce, boil it in a small saucepan for at least 1 minute before serving.
- Don't leave raw or cooked food lying in the sun.
- Use an instant-read thermometer to check the internal temperature of large pieces of meat, poultry or fish. Insert it sideways through the food to get an accurate reading.

Meat wave

Sliced Sirloin with
Rocket & Parmesan

serves 4

4 sirloin steaks, about 3 cm/
1¼ inches thick, 225 g/
8 oz each
olive oil, for brushing
100 g/3½ oz rocket
Parmesan shavings
balsamic vinegar, for drizzling
salt and pepper

Preheat the barbecue to high. Snip the fat on the steaks at 1-cm/½-inch intervals to stop it curling and shrinking. Sprinkle both sides with salt and pepper. Cover and leave to stand at room temperature for 30 minutes.

Heap some of the coals on one side leaving a slightly cooler zone with a single layer of coals. Oil the barbecue rack.

Cook the steaks on the hottest part of the grill for 2–3 minutes each side until brown. Move to the cooler part of the fire and cook to your liking: rare 2½ minutes, medium–rare 3–3½ minutes and medium 4 minutes. Transfer to a board and leave to rest for 5 minutes.

Divide the rocket between individual serving plates. Carve each steak diagonally into 2-cm/¾-inch slices. Place the slices on the rocket, keeping the steaks as close to the original shape as possible. Sprinkle with Parmesan shavings and more black pepper. Drizzle over a little balsamic vinegar and serve at once.

Burgers with
Chilli & Basil

serves 4

650 g/1 lb 7 oz minced beef
1 red pepper, deseeded and finely
  chopped
1 garlic clove, finely chopped
2 small red chillies, deseeded and
  finely chopped
1 tbsp chopped fresh basil,
  plus extra sprigs to garnish
½ tsp ground cumin
1 tbsp oil, for brushing
salt and pepper
hamburger buns, to serve

Preheat the barbecue to high.

Using a fork, lightly mix the beef, red pepper, garlic, chillies, chopped basil, cumin and salt and pepper to taste, until well combined. Divide the mixture into 4 balls and flatten into patties about 2.5 cm/1 inch thick. Season the outside with salt and pepper, and lightly brush with oil.

Oil the barbecue rack. Cook the burgers for 5 minutes on each side, or until cooked through. Brush the inside of the buns with oil and toast over the barbecue, cut-side down, for 1–2 minutes. Place the burgers in the buns and garnish with basil leaves.

Cheese & Bacon Burgers

serves 4

675 g/1 lb 8 oz freshly minced
    sirloin or rump steak
2 tbsp grated onion
1 tsp Worcestershire sauce
4 rashers streaky bacon
4 hamburger buns
olive oil, for brushing
4 thin squares Cheddar cheese
salt and pepper

toppings
shredded lettuce
red onion, thinly sliced
tomato, thinly sliced
gherkin, thinly sliced
mustard
tomato ketchup
mayonnaise

Preheat the barbecue to high.

Using a fork, lightly mix the beef with the onion, Worcestershire sauce, and salt and pepper to taste. Divide the mixture into balls and flatten into patties about 2.5 cm/ 1 inch thick. Season the outside with salt and pepper, and lightly brush with oil.

Oil the barbecue rack. Cook the bacon for 3–4 minutes, turning once. Set aside and keep warm. Cook the burgers for 5 minutes, then turn and place the cheese squares on top. Cook for a further 3–4 minutes. Brush the inside of the buns with oil and toast over the barbecue, cut-side down, for 1–2 minutes. Place the burgers in the buns, and add the bacon and chosen toppings.

Herb-crusted Beef Fillet with Horseradish Butter

serves 4

1 beef tenderloin, about 1 kg/
   2 lb 4 oz
1 tbsp olive oil
½ tbsp sea salt flakes
1 tsp coarsely ground black pepper
4 tbsp chopped fresh mixed herbs
   such as marjoram, thyme, sage,
   flat-leaf parsley

horseradish butter
100 g/3½ oz unsalted butter,
   at room temperature
3 tbsp grated fresh horseradish,
   or grated horseradish from a jar
salt and pepper

Put the meat in a shallow dish and brush all over with the olive oil. Sprinkle with the sea salt flakes, coarsely ground black pepper and herbs, rubbing in well. Cover and leave to marinate in the refrigerator for 2 hours. Allow to come to room temperature before cooking.

To make the horseradish butter, mash the butter with a fork until soft, then add the remaining ingredients, mixing well. Scrape the mixture onto a piece of clingfilm and form into a log. Wrap tightly and chill in the refrigerator.

Preheat the barbecue to medium–hot. Push some of the coals to one side to make a slightly cooler coal-free zone. Oil the barbecue rack.

Cook the meat for 8 minutes, giving it a quarter turn every 2 minutes, until brown and crusty on the outside. Move to the cooler part of the fire and cover with a lid. Cook for 16–18 minutes for rare (internal temperature 54°C/130°F) or 20–25 minutes for medium–rare (internal temperature 60°C/140°F). Use an instant-read thermometer to check the temperature.

Transfer the meat to a board. Cover with foil and leave for 15 minutes. Carve into 1-cm/½-inch diagonal slices, and arrange on warm serving plates. Serve with the juices that have flowed from the meat, and slices of horseradish butter.

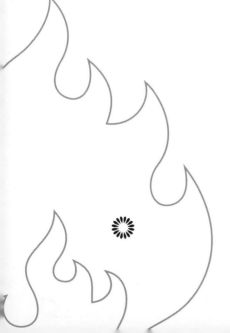

Beef Teriyaki

serves 4

450 g/1 lb extra thin beef steaks
1 yellow pepper, deseeded and cut
    into chunks
8 spring onions, trimmed and cut
    into short lengths
oil, for brushing
salad leaves, to serve

sauce
1 tsp cornflour
2 tbsp dry sherry
2 tbsp white wine vinegar
3 tbsp soy sauce
1 tbsp dark muscovado sugar
1 garlic clove, crushed
½ tsp ground cinnamon
½ tsp ground ginger

Place the beef steaks in a shallow, non-metallic dish. To make the sauce, mix the cornflour and sherry together in a small bowl, then stir in the remaining sauce ingredients. Pour the sauce over the meat, cover with clingfilm and leave to marinate in the refrigerator for at least 2 hours.

Preheat the barbecue to medium–hot and oil the barbecue rack. Remove the meat from the sauce and reserve. Pour the sauce into a small saucepan and boil for at least 5 minutes, stirring occasionally.

Cut the meat into thin strips and thread these, concertina-style, on to several presoaked wooden skewers, alternating each strip of meat with the pieces of pepper and spring onion. Cook the kebabs over hot coals for 5–8 minutes, turning and basting the beef and vegetables occasionally with the reserved sauce.

Arrange the skewers on serving plates and pour over the remaining sauce. Serve with salad leaves.

Beef with Wild Mushrooms

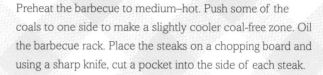

serves 4

oil, for brushing
4 beef steaks
50 g/1¾ oz butter
1–2 garlic cloves, crushed
150 g/5½ oz mixed wild
   mushrooms
2 tbsp chopped fresh parsley

to serve
salad leaves
cherry tomatoes, halved

Preheat the barbecue to medium–hot. Push some of the coals to one side to make a slightly cooler coal-free zone. Oil the barbecue rack. Place the steaks on a chopping board and using a sharp knife, cut a pocket into the side of each steak.

To make the stuffing, heat the butter in a large frying pan. Add the garlic and fry gently for 1 minute. Add the mushrooms to the frying pan and sauté gently for 4–6 minutes, or until tender. Remove the frying pan from the heat and stir in the parsley.

Divide the mushroom mixture into 4 and insert a portion into the pocket of each steak. Seal the pocket with a cocktail stick. If preparing ahead, allow the mixture to cool before stuffing the steaks.

Cook the steaks over hot coals, searing the meat over the hottest part of the barbecue for 2 minutes on each side. Move the steaks to the cooler area of the barbecue and cook for a further 4–10 minutes on each side, depending on how well done you like your steaks.

Transfer the steaks to serving plates and remove the cocktail sticks. Serve with salad leaves and cherry tomatoes.

Sichuan Peppered Steak

serves 4

4 flank steaks or thin rump steaks,
    about 175 g/6 oz each
oil for brushing
½ head Chinese leaves, thinly sliced
25 g/1 oz mint leaves
25 g/1 oz coriander leaves
½ red onion, thinly sliced
squeeze of lime juice
salt and pepper
lime wedges, to garnish

marinade
1 whole garlic bulb, cloves peeled
    and separated
¼ tsp salt
2 tbsp Sichuan peppercorns
1 tbsp black peppercorns
2 tsp soft brown sugar
1 Thai bird chilli, deseeded and
    finely chopped
4 tbsp soy sauce
juice of 1 lime

Place the steaks between two sheets of polythene and pound with a meat mallet until flattened to 5 mm/¼ inch. Slice each steak in half and place in a single layer in a shallow dish.

To make the marinade, pound the garlic with the salt using a roomy mortar and pestle. Add both types of peppercorn, the sugar and chilli, and pound to a paste. Stir in the soy sauce and lime juice. Pour over the meat, turning to coat. Cover with clingfilm and leave to marinate at room temperature for 1 hour, or preferably overnight in the refrigerator. Allow to come to room temperature before cooking.

Preheat the barbecue to medium–hot. Arrange the Chinese leaves, mint and coriander leaves in a shallow serving dish. Scatter with the onion slices and sprinkle with salt, black pepper and lime juice.

Remove the meat from the marinade, scraping off any solids and discarding the marinade. Pat dry with kitchen paper and lightly brush with oil. Thread concertina-style on to 4 skewers, allowing 2 strips of meat per skewer. Oil the barbecue rack.

Cook the meat for 3–4 minutes a side until browned. Transfer to a warm dish, remove the skewers and leave to rest for 5 minutes. Arrange on top of the salad and sprinkle with any juices that have flowed from the meat.

Steak Fajitas

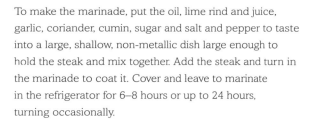

serves 4

1 piece of rump steak, about
    675 g/1 lb 8 oz and 2 cm/
    ¾ inch thick
4 wheat tortillas
1 avocado
2 tomatoes, thinly sliced
4 tbsp soured cream
salt and pepper
4 spring onions, thinly sliced

marinade

2 tbsp sunflower oil,
    plus extra for oiling
finely grated rind of 1 lime
1 tbsp lime juice
2 garlic cloves, crushed
¼ tsp ground coriander
¼ tsp ground cumin
pinch of sugar

To make the marinade, put the oil, lime rind and juice, garlic, coriander, cumin, sugar and salt and pepper to taste into a large, shallow, non-metallic dish large enough to hold the steak and mix together. Add the steak and turn in the marinade to coat it. Cover and leave to marinate in the refrigerator for 6–8 hours or up to 24 hours, turning occasionally.

Preheat the barbecue to medium–hot. Heap some of the hot coals on one side leaving a slightly cooler zone with a single layer of coals. Oil the barbecue rack. Using a slotted spoon, remove the steak from the marinade and place on the barbecue rack. Cook the steaks on the hottest part of the grill for 2–3 minutes each side until brown, basting once or twice with any remaining marinade. Move to the cooler part of the fire and cook to your liking: rare 2½ minutes, medium–rare 3–3½ minutes and medium 4 minutes. Transfer to a board and leave to rest for 5 minutes.

Meanwhile, warm the tortillas according to the instructions on the packet. Peel and slice the avocado.

Thinly slice the steak across the grain and arrange an equal quantity of the slices on one side of each tortilla. Add the tomato and avocado slices, top with a spoonful of soured cream and sprinkle over the spring onions. Fold over and eat at once.

Spiced Lamb & Apricot Kebabs

serves 4

675 g/1 lb 8 oz boneless lamb,
   cut into 2.5-cm/1-inch cubes
12 no-soak dried apricots, halved
   lengthways
6 baby onions, quartered
   lengthways
18 fresh bay leaves
oil for brushing
plain boiled rice, to serve

marinade
4 tbsp vegetable oil
2 onions, finely chopped
4 garlic cloves, finely chopped
2 tbsp curry powder
2 tsp garam masala
½ tsp cayenne pepper
2 tbsp muscovado sugar
1 tsp salt
1 tsp freshly ground black pepper
4 tbsp wine vinegar
5 tbsp apricot jam
200 ml/7 fl oz water

First make the marinade. Heat the oil in a frying pan over a medium heat. Add the onions and cook gently for 10 minutes or until browned. Add the garlic, curry powder, garam masala and cayenne pepper, and continue frying for 30 seconds. Stir in the sugar. salt, pepper, vinegar, apricot jam and half the water. Simmer, stirring for 2–3 minutes or until the marinade thickens. Remove from the heat and leave to cool completely.

Put the lamb in a bowl with the cold marinade, stirring to coat. Cover with clingfilm and leave to marinate in the refrigerator for at least 4 hours or overnight. Allow to come to room temperature before cooking.

Preheat the barbecue to medium–hot. Remove the meat from the marinade, reserving the marinade in a small saucepan. Thread the meat onto 6 skewers, alternating with the apricots, baby onions and bay leaves, and brush with oil. Oil the barbecue rack. Cook for 15 minutes, turning every 5 minutes and brushing with more oil.

Add the remaining water to the reserved marinade. Boil for 5 minutes, stirring constantly, until thickened. Serve the kebabs with the hot marinade and plain boiled rice.

Minty
Lamb Burgers

serves 4–6

oil for brushing
1 red pepper, deseeded and cut
    into quarters
1 yellow pepper, deseeded and cut
    into quarters
1 red onion, cut into thick wedges
1 baby aubergine (115 g/4 oz),
    cut into wedges
450 g/1 lb fresh lamb mince
2 tbsp freshly grated Parmesan
    cheese
1 tbsp chopped fresh mint
salt and pepper

minty mustard mayonnaise
4 tbsp mayonnaise
1 tsp Dijon mustard
1 tbsp chopped fresh mint

to serve
hamburger buns
shredded lettuce
grilled vegetables, such as peppers
    and cherry tomatoes

Preheat the barbecue to medium–hot. Oil the barbecue rack.

Place the peppers, onions and aubergine on the rack and cook over hot coals for 10–12 minutes, or until charred. Remove, leave to cool, then peel the peppers.

Place all the vegetables in a food processor and, using the pulse button, chop. Add the lamb mince, Parmesan cheese, chopped mint and salt and pepper to taste to the food processor and blend until combined. Divide the mixture into balls and flatten into patties about 2.5 cm/1 inch thick. Season the outside with salt and pepper, and lightly brush with oil.

Next make the minty mustard mayonnaise. Blend the mayonnaise with the mustard and chopped fresh mint. Cover and chill until required.

Place the burgers over hot coals and cook for 5 minutes on each side, or until cooked through. Brush the inside of the buns with oil and toast over the barbecue, cut-side down, for 1–2 minutes. Place the burgers in the buns with the shredded lettuce, prepared mayonnaise and barbecued vegetables.

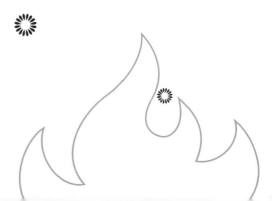

Moroccan
Lamb Burgers

serves 4

550 g/1 lb 4 oz minced lamb
1 onion, grated
1 tsp harissa sauce
1 garlic clove, crushed
2 tbsp finely chopped fresh mint
½ tsp cumin seeds, crushed
½ tsp paprika
oil for brushing
salt and pepper

yogurt & cucumber sauce

1 small ridge cucumber, or ½ large
   cucumber
4 tbsp natural yogurt
6 tbsp chopped fresh mint
salt and pepper

to serve

4 pitta breads, warmed
red onion, sliced
shredded lettuce
salt and pepper

To make the sauce, peel the cucumber, quarter lengthways and scoop out the seeds. Chop the flesh and put in a sieve set over a bowl. Sprinkle with salt, cover with a plate and weigh down with a can of vegetables. Leave to drain for 30 minutes, then mix with the remaining ingredients.

Combine the lamb, grated onion, harissa sauce, garlic, mint, cumin seeds and paprika. Season generously with salt and freshly ground black pepper, mixing well with a fork. Divide into 4 balls and flatten into patties about 2.5 cm/1 inch thick. Cover and leave to stand at room temperature for 30 minutes.

Preheat the barbecue to high. Lightly brush the burgers with oil and oil the barbecue rack. Cook for 5–6 minutes for medium.

Stuff the burgers into warm pitta breads, with some onion, shredded lettuce and a spoonful of the sauce. Serve the remaining sauce separately.

Butterflied Lamb with
Balsamic Vinegar & Mint

serves 4

1 boned leg of lamb,
   about 1.8 kg/4 lb
olive oil for brushing

marinade
8 tbsp balsamic vinegar
grated rind and juice of 1 lemon
150 ml/5 fl oz sunflower oil
4 tbsp chopped fresh mint
2 garlic cloves, crushed
2 tbsp light muscovado sugar
salt and pepper

to serve
barbecued vegetables, such as
   peppers and courgettes
black or green olives

Preheat the barbecue and oil the barbecue rack. Arrange the lamb so that its shape resembles a butterfly. Thread 2–3 skewers through the meat to make it easier to turn on the barbecue.

Mix the balsamic vinegar, lemon rind and juice, sunflower oil, mint, garlic, sugar and salt and pepper to taste together in a non-metallic dish that is large enough to hold the lamb. Place the lamb in the dish and turn it over a few times so that the meat is coated on both sides with the marinade. Cover and leave to marinate in the refrigerator for at least 6 hours, or preferably overnight, turning occasionally.

Preheat the barbecue and oil the barbecue rack. Remove the lamb from the marinade and reserve the liquid for basting. Place the rack about 15 cm/6 inches above the coals and cook the lamb for 30 minutes on each side, turning once and basting frequently with the marinade.

Transfer the lamb to a chopping board and remove the skewers. Cut the lamb into slices across the grain and serve with barbecued vegetables and olives.

Rack & Ruin

serves 4

4 racks of lamb, each with 4 cutlets
oil for brushing

marinade
2 tbsp extra virgin olive oil
1 tbsp balsamic vinegar
1 tbsp lemon juice
3 tbsp finely chopped
   fresh rosemary
1 small onion, finely chopped
salt and pepper

Place the racks of lamb in a large, shallow, non-metallic dish. Place the oil, vinegar, lemon juice, rosemary and onion in a jug and stir together. Season to taste with salt and pepper.

Pour the marinade over the lamb and turn until thoroughly coated. Cover with clingfilm and leave to marinate in the refrigerator for 1 hour, turning occasionally.

Preheat the barbecue and oil the barbecue rack. Cook over medium–hot coals for 10 minutes on each side, brushing frequently with the marinade. Serve immediately.

Spicy Lamb
Steaks

serves 4

4 lamb steaks, about
175 g/6 oz each
oil for brushing
8 fresh rosemary sprigs
8 fresh bay leaves
2 tbsp olive oil

spicy marinade
2 tbsp sunflower oil
1 large onion, finely chopped
2 garlic cloves, finely chopped
2 tbsp jerk seasoning
1 tbsp curry paste
1 tsp fresh ginger, grated
400 g/14 oz canned chopped
tomatoes
4 tbsp Worcestershire sauce
3 tbsp light muscovado sugar
salt and pepper

To make the marinade, heat the oil in a heavy-based saucepan. Add the onion and garlic and cook, stirring occasionally, for 5 minutes, or until softened. Stir in the jerk seasoning, curry paste and grated ginger and cook, stirring constantly, for 2 minutes. Add the tomatoes, Worcestershire sauce and sugar, then season to taste with salt and pepper. Bring to the boil, stirring constantly, then reduce the heat and simmer for 15 minutes, or until thickened. Remove from the heat and leave to cool.

Place the lamb steaks between 2 sheets of clingfilm and beat with the side of a rolling pin to flatten. Transfer the steaks to a large, shallow, non-metallic dish. Pour the marinade over them, turning to coat. Cover with clingfilm and leave to marinate in the refrigerator for 3 hours.

Preheat the barbecue and oil the barbecue rack. Drain the lamb, reserving the marinade. Cook the lamb over medium–hot coals, brushing frequently with the marinade, for 5–7 minutes on each side. Meanwhile, dip the rosemary and bay leaves in the olive oil and cook on the barbecue for 3–5 minutes. Serve the lamb immediately with the herbs.

 Honey-glazed
Pork chops

serves 4

4 lean pork loin chops
olive oil for brushing
salt and pepper

honey glaze
4 tbsp clear honey
1 tbsp dry sherry
4 tbsp orange juice
2 tbsp olive oil
2.5-cm/1-inch piece fresh ginger,
   grated

Preheat the barbecue and oil the barbecue rack. Season the pork chops with salt and pepper and set aside.

To make the glaze, place the honey, sherry, orange juice, olive oil and the ginger in a small saucepan. Bring to the boil, stirring constantly, then reduce the heat and simmer for 15 minutes, or until thickened. Remove from the heat and leave to cool.

Brush the pork chops with the oil and cook on the barbecue for 5 minutes on each side. Brush the chops with the glaze and cook for a further 2–4 minutes on each side, basting frequently with the glaze.

Transfer the pork chops to serving plates and serve immediately.

Jamaican Jerk
Pork Fillet

serves 4–6

2 pork fillets of equal length, about
1 kg/2 lb 4 oz in total
vegetable oil, for brushing
salt and pepper
plain boiled rice, to serve

jerk marinade
3 tbsp allspice berries
3 cloves
2-cm/3/4-inch piece cinnamon
stick, broken
½ tsp freshly grated nutmeg
2 large garlic cloves
1-2 fresh red chillies, deseeded and
finely chopped
large bunch of fresh chives, about
40 g/1½ oz, snipped
2 tsp sea salt
2 tbsp malt vinegar
2 tbsp soy sauce
1 tbsp rum

To make the marinade, dry-roast the allspice berries in a
small frying pan for a few seconds until you smell the aroma.
Using a mortar and pestle, grind to a powder with the cloves,
cinnamon stick and nutmeg. Tip into a food processor or
blender with the remaining marinade ingredients. Process to
a thin paste for 2 minutes, scraping the sides frequently.

Trim the sinew and narrow tips from the pork fillets, and pull
off any silvery skin. Spread the marinade all over the fillets,
rubbing it in well. Cover with clingfilm and leave to marinate
in the refrigerator for 2 hours.

Place the fillets on a board. Brush the two upward-facing
surfaces with oil. Place the other fillet on top, oiled-side
down, to make a sandwich. Tie neatly with string at
3.5-cm/1¼-inch intervals and brush all over with oil. Season
with salt and pepper. Cover and leave to stand at room
temperature for 30 minutes.

Preheat the barbecue to high. Heap some of the coals on
one side leaving a slightly cooler zone with a single layer of
coals. Oil the barbecue rack.

Cook the meat over a high heat for 8 minutes, giving it a
quarter turn every 2 minutes, until brown and crusty on the
outside. Move to the cooler part of the fire and cover with a
lid. Cook for 20-25 minutes, or until the internal temperature
reaches 60°C/140°F on an instant-read thermometer.

Transfer the meat to a board. Cover with foil and leave for
10 minutes. Carve into 1-cm/½-inch diagonal slices, and
arrange on warm serving plates. Serve with the juices that
have flowed from the meat, and plain boiled rice.

Meatballs on Sticks

serves 8

4 pork and herb sausages
115 g/4 oz fresh beef mince
85 g/3 oz fresh white breadcrumbs
1 onion, finely chopped
2 tbsp chopped mixed fresh herbs,
    such as parsley, thyme and sage
1 egg
sunflower oil, for brushing
salt and pepper

Preheat the barbecue to high. Soak the cocktail sticks in water for 30 minutes, to prevent burning.

Remove the sausage meat from the skins and place in a large bowl. Using a fork, lightly mix the sausage meat, beef mince, breadcrumbs, onion, herbs, egg and salt and pepper to taste, until well combined. Divide the mixture into 8 balls, about the size of a golf ball. Season the outside with salt and pepper, spear with a cocktail stick and lightly brush with oil.

Oil the barbecue rack. Cook the meatballs over the barbecue, for 10 minutes, or until cooked through, turning frequently and brushing with more oil if necessary. Transfer to a plate and serve.

Hot & Spicy Ribs

serves 4

olive oil for brushing
1 onion, chopped
2 garlic cloves, chopped
2.5-cm/1-inch piece fresh ginger,
    sliced
1 fresh red chilli, deseeded and
    chopped
5 tbsp dark soy sauce
3 tbsp lime juice
1 tbsp palm or muscovado sugar
2 tbsp groundnut oil
1 kg/2 lb 4 oz pork spare ribs,
    separated
salt and pepper

Preheat the barbecue to high and oil the barbecue rack. Put the onion, garlic, ginger, chilli and soy sauce into a food processor and process to a paste. Transfer to a jug and stir in the lime juice, sugar and oil and season to taste with salt and pepper.

Place the spare ribs in a preheated wok or large, heavy-based saucepan and pour in the soy sauce mixture. Place on the hob and bring to the boil, then simmer over a low heat, stirring frequently, for 30 minutes. If the mixture appears to be drying out, add a little water.

Remove the spare ribs, reserving the sauce. Cook the ribs over medium–hot coals, turning and basting frequently with the sauce, for 20–30 minutes. Transfer to a large serving plate and serve immediately.

Pork & Apple Brochettes

serves 4

450 g/1 lb pork fillet
olive oil for brushing
2 crisp eating apples
1 tbsp sunflower oil
crusty bread, to serve

marinade
300 ml/10 fl oz dry cider
1 tbsp finely chopped fresh sage
6 black peppercorns, crushed

Using a sharp knife, cut the pork into 2.5-cm/1-inch cubes, then place in a large, shallow, non-metallic dish. Mix the cider, sage and peppercorns together in a jug, pour the mixture over the pork and turn until thoroughly coated. Cover with clingfilm and leave to marinate in the refrigerator for 1–2 hours.

Preheat the barbecue to high and oil the barbecue rack. Drain the pork, reserving the marinade. Core the apples, but do not peel, then cut into wedges. Dip the apple wedges into the reserved marinade and thread on to several metal skewers, alternating with the cubes of pork. Stir the sunflower oil into the remaining marinade.

Cook the brochettes over medium–hot coals, turning and brushing frequently with the reserved marinade, for 12–15 minutes. Transfer to a large serving plate and, if you prefer, remove the meat and apples from the skewers before serving. Serve immediately with crusty bread.

Barbecued Pork &
Thyme Sausages

serves 4

1 garlic clove, finely chopped
1 onion, grated
1 small red chilli, deseeded and
  finely chopped
450 g/1 lb lean minced pork
50 g/1¾ oz almonds, toasted and
  ground
50 g/1¾ oz fresh breadcrumbs
1 tbsp finely chopped fresh thyme
salt and pepper
flour, for dusting
vegetable oil, for brushing

to serve
fresh finger rolls
slices of onion, lightly cooked
ketchup and/or mustard

Put the garlic, onion, chilli, pork, almonds, breadcrumbs and fresh thyme into a large bowl. Season well with salt and pepper and mix until well combined.

Using your hands, form the mixture into sausage shapes. Roll each sausage in a little flour, then transfer to a bowl, cover with clingfilm and refrigerate for 45 minutes.

Preheat the barbecue. Brush a piece of aluminium foil with oil, then put the sausages on the foil and brush them with a little more vegetable oil. Transfer the sausages and foil to the barbecue.

Barbecue over hot coals, turning the sausages frequently, for about 15 minutes, or until cooked right through. Serve with finger rolls, cooked sliced onion and tomato ketchup and/or mustard.

Lemon & Rosemary Pork Fillet
with Fennel Butter

serves 4

2 pork fillets of equal length, about
   1 kg/2 lb 4 oz in total
2 tsp sea salt flakes, plus extra
olive oil for brushing
2 large garlic cloves, crushed
2 tsp finely chopped fresh rosemary
2 tsp fennel seeds, crushed
1 tsp coarsely ground black pepper
coarsely grated zest of 1 lemon

fennel butter

2 tbsp fennel seeds
125 g/4½ oz unsalted butter
finely grated zest of ½ lemon
½ tsp freshly ground black pepper

Trim the sinew and narrow tips from the pork fillets, and pull off any silvery skin. Sprinkle with the 2 teaspoons of sea salt flakes, rubbing in well. Cover with clingfilm and leave in the refrigerator for 2 hours. Rinse and pat dry with kitchen paper.

To make the fennel butter, dry-fry the seeds in a small frying pan for a few seconds until the aroma is released. Grind to a coarse powder using a mortar and pestle. Mash the butter with a fork until soft, then add the fennel and remaining ingredients, mixing well. Scrape the mixture onto a piece of clingfilm and form into a log. Wrap tightly and chill in the refrigerator.

Place the fillets on a board. Brush the two upward-facing surfaces with olive oil. Combine the garlic, rosemary, fennel seeds, black pepper and lemon zest with another pinch of sea salt. Spread the mixture evenly over the upward-facing surface of one of the fillets. Place the other fillet on top, oiled-side down, to make a sandwich. Tie neatly with string at 3.5-cm/ 1¼ -inch intervals and brush all over with olive oil. Cover and leave to stand at room temperature for 30 minutes.

Preheat the barbecue to high. Heap some of the coals on one side leaving a slightly cooler zone with a single layer of coals. Oil the barbecue rack.

Cook the meat over a high heat for 8 minutes, giving it a quarter turn every 2 minutes, until brown and crusty on the outside. Move to the cooler part of the fire and cover with a lid. Cook for 20–25 minutes, or until the internal temperature reaches 60°C/140°F on an instant-read thermometer.

Transfer the meat to a board. Cover with foil and leave for 10 minutes. Carve into 1-cm/½-inch diagonal slices, and arrange on warm serving plates. Serve with the juices that have flowed from the meat, and slices of fennel butter.

Perfect Poultry

Barbecued Chicken
with Tarragon Butter

serves 4

4 skinless, boneless chicken breasts,
    about 225 g/8 oz each
olive oil for brushing

tarragon butter
100 g/3½ oz unsalted butter,
    at room temperature
5 tbsp chopped fresh tarragon
    (about 2 small packets)
1 shallot, finely chopped
salt and pepper

marinade
1½ tbsp lemon juice
2 tbsp water
1 tsp sugar
1 tsp salt
½ tsp freshly ground black pepper
3 tbsp olive oil

Preheat the barbecue. To make the tarragon butter, mash the butter with a fork until soft, then add the remaining ingredients, mixing well. Scrape the mixture onto a piece of clingfilm and form into a log. Wrap tightly and chill in the refrigerator.

Slice the chicken breasts lengthways to make 8 portions. Trim any excess fat and very thin pieces of flesh. Place in a single layer in a shallow dish. Whisk together the marinade ingredients and pour over the chicken. Cover with clingfilm and marinate for 30 minutes, turning halfway through.

Drain the chicken and discard the marinade. Pat dry and lightly brush with oil. Oil the barbecue rack. Place the chicken on the rack narrow-side down, and cover with a disposable foil tray. Grill over medium–hot coals for 5–6 minutes until the underside is striped with grill marks and is no longer translucent. Using tongs, turn and cook the other side for 4–5 minutes, or until evenly striped with grill marks and no longer pink when cut into (internal temperature 70°C/160°F).

Place in a warmed dish, cover with foil and leave to rest in a warm place for 5 minutes. Serve with slices of tarragon butter.

Spicy Chicken Wings

serves 4

16 chicken wings
sunflower oil, for brushing

marinade
4 tbsp sunflower oil
4 tbsp light soy sauce
5-cm/2-inch piece fresh ginger,
 roughly c hopped
2 garlic cloves, roughly chopped
juice and grated rind of 1 lemon
2 tsp ground cinnamon
2 tsp ground turmeric
4 tbsp clear honey
salt and pepper

sauce
2 orange peppers
2 yellow peppers
sunflower oil, for brushing
125 ml/4 fl oz natural yogurt
2 tbsp dark soy sauce
2 tbsp chopped fresh coriander

Place the chicken wings in a large, shallow, non-metallic dish. Put the oil, soy sauce, ginger, garlic, lemon rind and juice, cinnamon, turmeric and honey into a food processor and process to a smooth purée. Season to taste with salt and pepper. Spoon the mixture over the chicken wings and turn until thoroughly coated, cover with clingfilm and leave to marinate in the refrigerator for up to 8 hours.

Preheat the barbecue and oil the rack. To make the sauce, brush the peppers with the oil and cook over hot coals, turning frequently, for 10 minutes, or until the skin is blackened and charred. Remove from the barbecue and leave to cool slightly, then peel off the skins and discard the seeds. Put the flesh into a food processor with the yogurt and process to a smooth purée. Transfer to a bowl and stir in the soy sauce and chopped coriander.

Drain the chicken wings, reserving the marinade. Cook over medium–hot coals, turning and brushing frequently with the reserved marinade, for 8–10 minutes, or until thoroughly cooked. Serve immediately with the sauce.

Honey & Mustard Drumsticks

serves 4

8 chicken drumsticks
salad leaves, to serve

honey & mustard glaze
125 ml/4 fl oz clear honey
4 tbsp dijon mustard
4 tbsp wholegrain mustard
4 tbsp white wine vinegar
2 tbsp sunflower oil
salt and pepper

Using a sharp knife, make 2–3 diagonal slashes in the chicken drumsticks and place in a large, non-metallic dish.

Mix all the ingredients for the glaze together in a jug and season to taste with salt and pepper. Pour the glaze over the drumsticks, turning until the drumsticks are well coated. Cover with clingfilm and leave to marinate in the refrigerator for at least 1 hour.

Preheat the barbecue. Drain the chicken drumsticks, reserving the marinade. Cook the chicken over medium–hot coals, turning frequently and brushing with the reserved marinade, for 25–30 minutes, or until thoroughly cooked. Transfer to serving plates and serve immediately with the salad leaves.

Chicken Fajitas

serves 4

2–3 skinless, boneless chicken
    breasts, about 450 g/1 lb in total
1 Spanish onion
2 red or yellow peppers, deseeded
    and quartered lengthways
olive oil for brushing
3 tbsp chopped fresh coriander
4 corn tortillas, 19 cm/7½ inches
    diameter
salt and pepper
soured cream, to serve
Avocado Salsa (page 74), to serve

marinade
1 large garlic clove, crushed
½ –1 fresh green chilli, deseeded
    and finely chopped
½ tsp cumin seeds
1 tsp sugar
2 tbsp lime juice
2 tbsp white wine vinegar
4 tbsp olive oil
salt and pepper

Slice the chicken breasts horizontally in half to make
4–6 thinner pieces. Place between two sheets of polythene
and pound with a meat mallet until flattened to 5 mm/
¼ inch. Place in a single layer in a shallow dish.

To make the marinade, pound the garlic, chilli, cumin seeds,
sugar, salt and pepper to a paste using a mortar and pestle.
Transfer to a medium bowl and whisk in the lime juice,
wine vinegar and olive oil. Reserve 4 tablespoons of the
marinade and set aside. Pour the remaining marinade over
the chicken. Cover and leave to marinate for 30 minutes.
Preheat the barbecue.

Thickly slice the onion horizontally into three rounds. Insert
3–4 wooden cocktail sticks from the outer edge to the centre
of each round to keep the rings in place. Brush both sides
of the rounds and the quartered peppers with olive oil, and
arrange in a hinged wire grill basket.

Grill the vegetables over medium–hot coals for 8–12 minutes,
turning every 3–4 minutes, until tender-crisp and slightly
charred. Slice the peppers into thin strips and remove the
cocktail sticks from the onions. Tip the vegetables into a
warm bowl and toss with half the reserved marinade and
half the coriander. Cover with foil and keep warm.

Remove the chicken from the marinade, discarding the
marinade. Pat dry and lightly brush with oil. Oil the barbecue
rack. Cook for 3–4 minutes a side until no longer pink when
cut into with a small vegetable knife. Slice into thin strips,
put in a warm bowl, and toss with the remaining reserved
marinade and coriander. Cover with foil and keep warm.

Warm the tortillas either on the barbecue over medium–low
coals, or in a low oven. Spoon a little soured cream down
the middle of a warmed tortilla, and add some chicken and
vegetables. Roll up and serve with the salsa.

Zesty Kebabs

serves 4

4 skinless, boneless chicken breasts,
    about 175 g/6 oz each
citrus zest, to garnish

marinade
finely grated rind and juice of
    ½ lemon
finely grated rind and juice of
    ½ orange
2 tbsp clear honey
2 tbsp olive oil
2 tbsp chopped fresh mint,
    plus extra to garnish
¼ tsp ground coriander
salt and pepper

Using a sharp knife, cut the chicken into 2.5-cm/1-inch cubes, then place them in a large glass bowl. Place the lemon rind and orange rind, the lemon juice and orange juice, the honey, oil, mint and ground coriander in a jug and mix together. Season to taste with salt and pepper. Pour the marinade over the chicken cubes and toss until they are thoroughly coated. Cover with clingfilm and leave to marinate in the refrigerator for up to 8 hours.

Preheat the barbecue. Drain the chicken cubes, reserving the marinade. Thread the chicken on to several long metal skewers.

Cook the skewers over medium–hot coals, turning and brushing frequently with the reserved marinade, for 6–10 minutes, or until thoroughly cooked. Transfer to a large serving plate, garnish with fresh chopped mint and citrus zest and serve immediately.

Spicy Tomato Kebabs

serves 4

500 g/1 lb 2 oz skinless, boneless
   chicken breasts
250 g/9 oz cherry tomatoes
olive oil for brushing

glaze
3 tbsp tomato purée
2 tbsp clear honey
2 tbsp Worcestershire sauce
1 tbsp chopped fresh rosemary

Preheat the barbecue to high. Soak four wooden skewers in water for 30 minutes, to prevent burning.

Using a sharp knife, cut the chicken into small pieces and place in a bowl. Using a fork, lightly mix the tomato purée, honey, Worcestershire sauce and rosemary until the chicken is evenly coated. Thread the chicken pieces and cherry tomatoes alternately onto the wooden skewers.

Oil the barbecue rack. Cook the kebabs over medium–hot coals, turning and brushing frequently with any remaining glaze, for 6–10 minutes, or until thoroughly cooked. Transfer to a plate and serve.

Chicken Satay Skewers

serves 4

4 tbsp smooth peanut butter
100 ml/3½ fl oz soy sauce
4 skinless, boneless chicken breasts,
    cut into thin strips
olive oil for brushing

Preheat the barbecue to high. Soak four wooden skewers in water for 30 minutes, to prevent burning.

Using a fork, mix together the peanut butter and soy sauce in a bowl until smooth. Stir in the chicken strips, and mix until evenly coated. Thread the chicken strips onto wooden skewers.

Oil the barbecue rack. Cook the skewers over medium–hot coals, turning frequently, for 6–10 minutes, or until thoroughly cooked. Transfer to a plate and serve.

Cajun Chicken

serves 4

4 chicken drumsticks
4 chicken thighs
2 fresh corn cobs, husks and silks
    removed
85 g/3 oz butter, melted

spice mix
2 tsp onion powder
2 tsp paprika
1½ tsp salt
1 tsp garlic powder
1 tsp dried thyme
1 tsp cayenne pepper
1 tsp ground black pepper
½ tsp ground white pepper
¼ tsp ground cumin

Preheat the barbecue. Using a sharp knife, make
2–3 diagonal slashes in the chicken drumsticks and thighs,
then place them in a large dish. Cut the corn cobs into thick
slices and add them to the dish. Mix all the ingredients for
the spice mix together in a small bowl.

Brush the chicken and corn with the melted butter and
sprinkle with the spice mix. Toss to coat well.

Cook the chicken over medium–hot coals, turning
occasionally, for 15 minutes, then add the corn slices and
cook, turning occasionally, for a further 10–15 minutes, or
until beginning to blacken slightly at the edges. Transfer to a
large serving plate and serve immediately.

Butterflied Poussins

serves 4

4 poussins, about 450 g / 1 lb each
fresh coriander sprigs, to garnish
corn on the cob, to serve

marinade
1 tbsp paprika
1 tbsp mustard powder
1 tbsp ground cumin
pinch of cayenne pepper
1 tbsp tomato ketchup
1 tbsp lemon juice
salt
5 tbsp melted butter

To butterfly the poussins, turn 1 bird breast-side down and, using strong kitchen scissors or poultry shears, cut through the skin and ribcage along both sides of the backbone, from tail to neck. Remove the backbone and turn the bird breast-side up. Press down firmly on the breastbone to flatten. Fold the wingtips underneath. Push a skewer through one wing, the top of the breast and out of the other wing. Push a second skewer through one thigh, the bottom of the breast and out through the other thigh. Repeat with the remaining poussins.

Mix the paprika, mustard powder, cumin, cayenne, tomato ketchup and lemon juice together in a small bowl and season to taste with salt. Gradually stir in the butter to make a smooth paste. Spread the paste evenly over the poussins, cover and leave to marinate in the refrigerator for up to 8 hours.

Preheat the barbecue. Cook the poussins over medium–hot coals, turning frequently, for 25–30 minutes, brushing with a little oil if necessary. Transfer to a serving plate, garnish with fresh coriander sprigs and serve with corn on the cob

Chicken
Burgers

serves 4

4 large chicken breast fillets,
    skinned
1 large egg white
1 tbsp cornflour
1 tbsp plain flour
1 egg, beaten
55 g/2 oz fresh white breadcrumbs
2 tbsp sunflower oil
2 beef tomatoes, sliced

to serve
hamburger buns
shredded lettuce
mayonnaise

Place the chicken breasts between 2 sheets of non-stick baking paper and flatten slightly using a meat mallet or a rolling pin. Beat the egg white and cornflour together, then brush over the chicken. Cover and leave to chill for 30 minutes, then coat in the flour.

Place the egg and breadcrumbs in 2 separate bowls and coat the burgers first in the egg, allowing any excess to drip back into the bowl, then in the breadcrumbs.

Preheat the barbecue. Lightly brush each burger with a little oil and then add them to the barbecue grill, cooking over medium–hot coals for 6–8 minutes on each side, or until thoroughly cooked. If you are in doubt, it is worth cutting one of the burgers in half. If there is any sign of pinkness, cook for a little longer to get that nice barbecue taste. Add the tomato slices to the grill rack for the last 1–2 minutes of the cooking time to heat through. Serve the burgers in hamburger buns with the shredded lettuce, cooked tomato slices and mayonnaise.

Turkey Tikka Kebabs

serves 4

4 thick turkey breast steaks,
    500 g/1 lb 2oz in total
½ tsp salt
½ tsp freshly ground black pepper
½–1 tsp cayenne pepper
juice of ½ lemon
12 bay leaves
4 small red onions, quartered
    lengthways
oil for brushing
1 tbsp chopped fresh coriander
lemon quarters, to garnish

marinade
175 g/6 oz Greek-style yogurt
5-cm/2-inch piece fresh ginger,
    chopped
1 tsp garam masala
½–1 tsp cayenne pepper
1 tsp salt
juice of ½ lemon
4 tbsp vegetable oil

Cut the turkey into cubes and put in a shallow dish. Combine the salt, black pepper, cayenne and lemon juice in a small bowl, and pour over the turkey, turning to coat. Cover with clingfilm and leave to stand for 30 minutes.

Purée the marinade ingredients in a blender. Mix with the turkey, making sure the cubes are well coated. Cover and leave to marinate in the refrigerator for at least 2 hours or overnight. Allow to come to room temperature before cooking.

Preheat the barbecue. Thread the turkey cubes on to 4 skewers, alternating them with bay leaves and the large outer pieces of red onion (use the smaller bits in another recipe). Brush with oil on all sides. Oil the barbecue rack.

Cook the kebabs over medium–hot coals for 10–12 minutes, rotating them from time to time, until the turkey is cooked through and slightly charred at the edges. Transfer to a warm serving platter, sprinkle with the coriander and garnish with lemon quarters.

Mexican Turkey Steak with Avocado Salsa

serves 4

4 turkey steaks, 500 g/1 lb 2 oz
    in total
olive oil for brushing
warm tortillas, to serve

marinade
juice of 1 orange
juice of 2 limes
2 garlic cloves, crushed
1 tsp paprika
½ tsp salt
½ tsp chilli powder
½ tsp cumin seeds, crushed
¼ tsp freshly ground black pepper
4 tbsp olive oil

avocado salsa
2 avocados, finely diced
juice of 1 lime
1 small red onion, finely diced
1 tbsp chopped fresh coriander
salt

Halve the turkey steaks horizontally to make 8 thinner pieces. Place between two sheets of polythene and pound with a meat mallet until flattened to 1 cm/½ inch thick. Slice into strips about 4 cm/1½ inches wide and 6 cm/2½ inches long. Place in a single layer in a shallow dish.

Whisk together the marinade ingredients and pour over the turkey. Cover with clingfilm and leave in the refrigerator to marinate for at least 4 hours or overnight. Allow to come to room temperature before cooking.

Preheat the barbecue. Carefully toss the salsa ingredients together and leave to stand at room temperature to allow the flavours to develop.

Drain the turkey, discarding the marinade. Lightly brush with oil and thread concertina-style onto skewers. Oil the barbecue rack. Grill for 2–2½ minutes a side over hot coals until no longer pink when cut into with a small vegetable knife. Remove from the skewers and serve with the avocado salsa and warm tortillas.

Tarragon
Turkey

serves 4

4 turkey breasts, about 175 g/
    6 oz each
4 tsp wholegrain mustard
8 fresh tarragon sprigs, plus extra
    to garnish
4 smoked back bacon rashers
salt and pepper
salad leaves, to serve

Preheat the barbecue. Season the turkey to taste with salt and pepper, and, using a round-bladed knife, spread the mustard evenly over the turkey.

Place 2 tarragon sprigs on top of each turkey breast and wrap a bacon rasher around it to hold the herbs in place. Secure with a cocktail stick.

Cook the turkey over medium–hot coals for 5–8 minutes on each side. Transfer to serving plates and garnish with tarragon sprigs. Serve with salad leaves.

Turkey Skewers with
Coriander Pesto

serves 4

450 g/1 lb skinless, boneless turkey,
    cut into 5-cm/2-inch cubes
2 courgettes, thickly sliced
1 red and 1 yellow pepper,
    deseeded and cut into
    5-cm/2-inch squares
8 cherry tomatoes
8 baby onions, peeled but left
    whole

marinade
6 tbsp olive oil
3 tbsp dry white wine
1 tsp green peppercorns, crushed
2 tbsp chopped fresh coriander
salt

coriander pesto
55 g/2 oz fresh coriander leaves
15 g/½ oz fresh parsley leaves
1 garlic clove
55 g/2 oz pine kernels
25 g/1 oz freshly grated Parmesan
    cheese
6 tbsp extra virgin olive oil
juice of 1 lemon

Place the turkey in a large glass bowl. To make the marinade, mix the olive oil, wine, peppercorns and coriander together in a jug and season to taste with salt. Pour the mixture over the turkey and turn until the turkey is thoroughly coated. Cover with clingfilm and leave to marinate in the refrigerator for 2 hours.

Preheat the barbecue. To make the pesto, put the coriander and parsley into a food processor and process until finely chopped. Add the garlic and pine kernels and pulse until chopped. Add the Parmesan cheese, oil and lemon juice and process briefly to mix. Transfer to a bowl, cover and leave to chill in the refrigerator until required.

Drain the turkey, reserving the marinade. Thread the turkey, courgette slices, pepper pieces, cherry tomatoes and onions alternately on to metal skewers. Cook over medium–hot coals, turning and brushing frequently with the marinade, for 10 minutes. Serve immediately with the coriander pesto.

Spicy Turkey &
Sausage Kebabs

makes 8

6 tbsp olive oil
2 garlic cloves, crushed
1 fresh red chilli, deseeded and
    chopped
350 g/12 oz turkey breast fillet
300 g/10½ oz chorizo sausage
1 dessert apple
1 tbsp lemon juice
8 bay leaves
salt and pepper

Place the olive oil, garlic, chilli and salt and pepper to taste in a small screw-top jar and shake well to combine. Leave to stand for 1 hour for the garlic and chilli to flavour the oil.

Preheat the barbecue. Using a sharp knife, cut the turkey into 2.5-cm/1-inch pieces. Cut the sausage into 2.5-cm/1-inch lengths. Cut the apple into chunks and remove the core. Toss the apple in the lemon juice to prevent discoloration.

Thread the turkey and sausage pieces on to 8 metal skewers, alternating with the apple chunks and bay leaves.

Cook the kebabs over hot coals for 15 minutes, or until the turkey is cooked through. Turn and baste the kebabs frequently with the flavoured oil.

Transfer the kebabs to warmed serving plates and serve immediately.

Duck Kebabs with
Hoisin Sauce

serves 4–6

4 duck breasts, about 675 g/
   1 lb 8 oz in total
12 thin slices fresh ginger from the
   fattest part of the root

marinade
3 tbsp hoisin sauce
1 tbsp sugar
1 tbsp dry sherry or Chinese rice
   wine
2 tsp soy sauce
½ tsp salt
¼ tsp Chinese five-spice powder

Trim the duck breasts of excess fat and skin, and cut into
2.5-cm/1-inch cubes. Place in a shallow dish. Whisk together
the marinade ingredients and pour over the duck. Cover with
clingfilm and leave to marinate in the refrigerator for at least
4 hours or overnight. Allow to come to room temperature
before cooking.

Preheat the barbecue. Thread the duck cubes onto
6 skewers, interspersing with the ginger slices. Oil the
barbecue rack. Cook the kebabs over medium–hot coals for
15–20 minutes, rotating them every 5 minutes until browned
on the outside and still slightly pink in the middle.

Remove from the skewers and place in a warmed dish.
Cover with foil and leave to rest in a warm place for
5 minutes before serving.

Grilled Duck Breasts with
Spring Onion & Chinese Plum Sauce

serves 4

4 boneless duck breasts, about
    175 g/6 oz each
6 tbsp Chinese plum sauce
2 tbsp hoisin sauce
juice of ½ small orange
salt and pepper
shredded spring onions, to garnish

Place the duck breasts skin-side down on a board. Lift the edge of the fatty skin away from the flesh, and trim off about 1 cm/½ inch all round so that the skin is slightly narrower than the flesh. Turn skin-side up and make three diagonal slashes in the skin, but not all the way through to the flesh. Season both sides with salt and pepper and place in a single layer in a shallow dish.

Mix together the plum sauce, hoisin sauce and orange juice. Pour this over the duck breasts, turning to coat. Cover with clingfilm and leave to marinate for 30 minutes at room temperature or for 2 hours or more in the refrigerator. Allow to come to room temperature before cooking.

Preheat the barbecue to medium–hot. Remove the duck breasts from the marinade, scraping off and reserving the marinade. Place on the grill skin-side down, and cook over medium–hot coals for 2–3 minutes. Turn skin-side up, brush with the marinade, and cook for 8 minutes, turning and brushing halfway through. Turn skin-side up and cook for a further 2 minutes for medium–rare (internal temperature 60°C/140°F) or 4 minutes for medium (internal temperature 70°C/160°F). Use an instant-read thermometer to check the temperature.

Transfer the duck breasts to a warmed dish. Cover with foil and leave to rest in a warm place for 10 minutes – the meat will continue to cook as it rests.

Pour the remaining marinade into a small saucepan. Bring to the boil and boil for 1 minute.

Carve the breasts into 1-cm/½-inch diagonal slices, and arrange on serving plates. Pour over the cooked marinade and garnish with shredded spring onions.

Fruity Duck

serves 4

4 duck breasts
115 g/4 oz ready-to-eat dried
    apricots
2 shallots, thinly sliced
2 tbsp clear honey
1 tsp sesame oil
2 tsp Chinese five-spice powder

Preheat the barbecue. Using a sharp knife, cut a long slit in the fleshy side of each duck breast to make a pocket. Divide the apricots and shallots between the pockets and secure with skewers.

Mix the honey and sesame oil together in a small bowl and brush all over the duck. Sprinkle with the Chinese five-spice powder.

Cook the duck over medium–hot coals for 6–8 minutes on each side. Remove the skewers, transfer to a large serving plate and serve immediately.

Duck Leg with Honey Glaze & Mango Relish

serves 4

4 duck legs, about 250 g/9 oz each
4 very thin slices of lime, each cut
    into 4 segments
4 tbsp clear honey
juice of 1 lime
½ tsp salt
½ tsp freshly ground black pepper
2 tsp toasted sesame oil
lime wedges, to garnish

mango & chilli salsa
1 ripe mango, finely diced
juice of 1 lime
½ small red onion, finely diced
½ –1 red chilli, deseeded and
    finely diced
thumb-sized piece fresh ginger,
    squeezed in a garlic press
6 tbsp chopped fresh coriander
1 tsp sugar
½ tsp sea salt flakes

First make the salsa. Combine all the ingredients in a serving bowl. Cover with clingfilm and leave to stand at room temperature for 1 hour to allow the flavours to develop.

Preheat the barbecue. Remove excess lumps of fat from the duck legs, and prick the skin all over with a fork. Put in a colander and douse with a kettleful of boiling water to encourage the subcutaneous fat to flow. Pat dry with kitchen paper. Make 4 slashes in each leg and insert the lime segments, pushing them well in. Combine the honey, lime juice, salt, pepper and sesame oil, mixing well. Brush all over the duck legs.

Oil the barbecue rack. Rake the coals into two heaps on either side of the barbecue, and place a disposable foil drip pan in the middle. Place the duck legs skin-side down on the rack over the drip tray. Cover and cook over medium coals for 5 minutes, then turn and brush with the glaze. Continue to cook for 15 minutes, covered, turning every 5 minutes and brushing with the glaze. Turn skin-side up and cook for a further 2–3 minutes for medium–rare (internal temperature 60°C/140°F) or 4–5 minutes for medium (internal temperature 70°C/160°F). Use an instant-read thermometer to check the temperature.

Transfer the duck legs to a warmed serving dish. Cover with foil and leave to rest in a warm place for 10 minutes – the meat will continue to cook as it rests. Garnish with lime wedges and serve with the salsa.

Fishy Business

Barbecued Tuna with
Chilli-ginger Sauce

serves 4

4 tuna steaks, 2 cm/¾ inch thick,
   about 175 g/6 oz each
2 tbsp olive oil
salt
lime wedges to serve

ginger & chilli sauce
100 g/3½ oz soft brown sugar
125 ml/4 fl oz water
2.5-cm/1-inch piece of fresh ginger
1 green chilli, deseeded and finely
   chopped
1 large garlic clove, crushed
juice of ½ lime

Put the tuna steaks in a shallow dish in which they sit snugly in a single layer. Rub with salt and the olive oil.

To make the sauce, put the sugar and water in a small saucepan and bring to the boil. Boil for 7–8 minutes until syrupy. Add the ginger, chilli, garlic and lime, and boil for another minute. Pour into a bowl and leave until completely cold.

Pour the cold sauce over the tuna steaks, turning to coat. Cover with clingfilm and leave to marinate in the refrigerator for 30–60 minutes, turning occasionally.

Oil the barbecue rack and a hinged wire grill basket, using a wad of oil-soaked kitchen paper. Place the tuna steaks in the basket, reserving the marinade. Cook over hot coals for 2 minutes. Turn and cook the other side for 1 minute. Remove from the basket and keep warm.

Pour the reserved marinade into a small saucepan. Bring to the boil and boil for 2 minutes. Pour into a small jug. Arrange the steaks on warm plates and serve with lime wedges and the hot marinade.

Tuna with Chilli Salsa

serves 4

4 tuna steaks, about 175 g/
   6 oz each
grated rind and juice of 1 lime
2 tbsp olive oil
salt and pepper
fresh coriander sprigs, to garnish
lettuce leaves, to garnish
crusty bread, to serve

chilli salsa
2 orange peppers
1 tbsp olive oil
juice of 1 lime
juice of 1 orange
2–3 fresh red chillies, deseeded and
   chopped
pinch of cayenne pepper

Rinse the tuna thoroughly under cold running water and pat dry with kitchen paper, then place in a large, shallow, non-metallic dish. Sprinkle with the lime rind and pour the juice and olive oil over the fish. Season to taste with salt and pepper, cover with clingfilm and leave to marinate in the refrigerator for up to 1 hour.

Preheat the barbecue. To make the salsa, brush the peppers with the olive oil and cook over hot coals, turning frequently, for 10 minutes, or until the skin is blackened and charred. Remove from the barbecue and leave to cool slightly, then peel off the skins and discard the seeds. Put the peppers into a food processor with the remaining salsa ingredients and process to a purée. Transfer to a bowl and season to taste with salt and pepper.

Cook the tuna over hot coals for 4–5 minutes on each side, until golden. Transfer to serving plates, garnish with coriander sprigs and lettuce leaves, and serve with the salsa and plenty of crusty bread.

Tuna & Vegetable Kebabs

serves 4

4 tuna steaks, about 140 g/
     5 oz each
2 red onions
12 cherry tomatoes
1 red pepper, deseeded and diced
     into 2.5-cm/1-inch pieces
1 yellow pepper, deseeded and
     diced into 2.5-cm/1-inch pieces
1 courgette, sliced
1 tbsp chopped fresh oregano
4 tbsp olive oil
salt and pepper
lime wedges, to garnish
salad greens, to serve

Preheat the barbecue to high. Soak four wooden skewers in water for 30 minutes, to prevent burning.

Using a sharp knife, cut the tuna into 2.5-cm/1-inch pieces. Peel the onions and cut each onion lengthways into 6 wedges. Thread the tuna and vegetables alternately onto the wooden skewers and set aside. Mix the oregano and oil together in a small bowl. Season with salt and pepper and lightly brush the kebabs with oil.

Oil the barbecue rack. Cook the kebabs over medium–hot coals, turning frequently, for 6–10 minutes, or until thoroughly cooked. Transfer to a plate and serve with lime wedges and salad greens.

Salmon & Dill Cakes with Aioli

makes 8 cakes

300 g/10½ oz cooked salmon,
    flaked
300 g/10½ oz mashed potato
8 tbsp fresh dill, chopped
6 spring onions, some green part
    included, finely chopped
1 tbsp coarsely grated lemon zest
1 tbsp cornflour, sifted
1 tsp salt
½ tsp freshly ground black pepper
2 eggs, lightly beaten
flour for dusting
oil for brushing

aioli
3 large garlic cloves, peeled
1 tsp sea salt flakes
2 egg yolks, at room temperature
250 ml/9 fl oz extra virgin olive oil
2 tbsp lemon juice
salt

In a large bowl, combine the salmon, potato, dill, spring onions and lemon zest, mixing lightly with a fork. Sprinkle with the cornflour, salt and pepper, then stir in the beaten egg. With floured hands, form into 8 patties about 2 cm/¾ inch thick. Place on a greaseproof paper-lined tray and chill for at least 2 hours.

Preheat the barbecue. To make the aioli, crush the garlic cloves with the sea salt, using a mortar and pestle, to make a smooth paste. Transfer to a large bowl. Beat in the egg yolks. Add the oil, a few drops at a time, whisking constantly, until the mixture is thick and smooth. Beat in the lemon juice. Transfer to a serving bowl, cover with clingfilm and set aside.

Oil the barbecue rack and a hinged wire grill basket, using a wad of oil-soaked kitchen paper. Brush the patties with oil on both sides, and arrange in the basket. Cook over medium–hot coals, covered, for 8 minutes until golden. Turn and cook the other side, covered for 4–5 minutes until golden. Serve with the aioli.

Salmon & Artichoke Parcels

serves 4

4 salmon steaks, about 175 g/
    6 oz each
½ lemon, sliced
1 onion, sliced into rings
4 fresh dill sprigs
4 canned artichoke hearts, drained
4 tbsp olive oil
4 tbsp chopped fresh flat-leaf
    parsley
salt and pepper

Preheat the barbecue. Cut out 4 squares of double-thickness aluminium foil, each large enough to enclose a fish steak. Place the salmon on the foil and top with the lemon slices, onion rings and dill sprigs. Place an artichoke heart on each salmon steak.

Fold up the sides of the foil. Sprinkle 1 tablespoon of olive oil and 1 tablespoon of parsley into each parcel and season with a little salt and pepper. Fold over the edges of the foil securely.

Cook the fish parcels over hot coals for 15 minutes, turning once. Transfer the fish parcels to plates and unwrap. Serve immediately.

Salmon with Mango salsa

serves 4

4 salmon steaks, about 175 g/
   6 oz each
finely grated rind
   and juice of 1 lime or
   ½ lemon
salt and pepper

mango salsa
1 large mango, peeled, stoned and
   diced
1 red onion, finely chopped
2 passion fruit
2 fresh basil sprigs
2 tbsp lime juice
salt

Preheat the barbecue. Rinse the salmon steaks under cold running water, pat dry with kitchen paper and place in a large, shallow, non-metallic dish. Sprinkle with the lime rind and pour the juice over them. Season to taste with salt and pepper, cover and leave to stand while you make the salsa.

Place the mango flesh in a bowl with the onion. Cut the passion fruit in half and scoop out the seeds and pulp with a teaspoon into the bowl. Tear the basil leaves and add them to the bowl with the lime juice. Season to taste with salt and stir well. Cover with clingfilm and reserve until required.

Cook the salmon steaks over medium–hot coals for 3–4 minutes on each side. Serve immediately with the salsa.

Herb-stuffed Trout with Watercress Sauce

serves 4

4 whole trout, about 350 g / 12 oz
    each, cleaned
olive oil for brushing
1 small bunch flat-leaf parsley
1 small bunch chives
1 lemon, thinly sliced
salt and pepper
lemon wedges, to serve

watercress sauce
2 bunches watercress, coarse stalks
    discarded, roughly chopped
juice of ½ lemon
3 tbsp vegetable or fish stock
¼ tsp salt
¼ tsp freshly ground black pepper
4 tbsp double cream
4 tbsp Greek-style yogurt

Preheat the barbecue. Remove the heads from the trout and make two diagonal slashes on each side in the thickest part of the flesh, about 9 cm / 3½ inches apart. Brush all over with olive oil. Stuff the slashes and the body cavity with parsley sprigs, chives and half slices of lemon. Season with salt and pepper. Oil a hinged wire basket and place the trout in it.

Put the watercress, lemon juice, stock, salt and pepper in a food processor. Purée for 2–3 minutes, scraping down the sides of the bowl frequently. Pour into a jug, stir in the cream and yogurt and mix well.

Oil the barbecue rack. Cook the trout over hot coals for 5–6 minutes a side, or until the thickest part along the spine is opaque when cut into with a small vegetable knife.

Carefully remove the trout from the basket, using the tip of a knife to ease the skin away from the wire. Serve on warmed plates with lemon wedges and the watercress sauce.

Swordfish Steaks
with Coconut Glaze

serves 4

4 swordfish steaks, 2 cm/¾ inch
    thick, about 175 g/6 oz each
2 tbsp olive oil
sea salt flakes
1 tbsp chopped fresh coriander,
    to garnish

coconut glaze

425 ml/15 fl oz can Coco Lopez
    cream of coconut
125 ml/4 fl oz rum
4 tbsp soy sauce
1 tbsp black peppercorns, cracked
5-cm/2-inch piece cinnamon stick,
    broken

Put the swordfish steaks in a shallow dish in which they sit snugly in a single layer. Rub with sea salt flakes and olive oil.

Put the coconut glaze ingredients in a small saucepan and bring to the boil, stirring. Boil for 12–15 minutes until reduced by half. Strain, pour into a shallow dish and leave until completely cold.

Pour the glaze over the swordfish, turning to coat and making sure the steaks are completely covered with the glaze. Cover with clingfilm and leave to marinate in the refrigerator for 30–60 minutes.

Preheat the barbecue. Grease the grill grate and a hinged wire grill basket, using a wad of oil-soaked kitchen paper. Drain the steaks, reserving the marinade. Brush the steaks with oil on both sides, and arrange in the basket. Cook over medium–hot coals, covered, for 5–6 minutes until blackened. Turn and cook the other side for 1 minute, or until the flesh is no longer opaque.

Meanwhile, pour the marinade into a small saucepan. Bring to the boil and boil for 3 minutes. Pour into a small jug.

Carefully remove the steaks from the basket. Arrange in a warm serving dish, sprinkle with the coriander, and serve with the coconut glaze.

Baked Snapper

serves 4

2 bunches fresh basil
85 g/3 oz butter, softened
4 garlic cloves, crushed
4 red snapper or red mullet, about
    350 g/12 oz each, scaled,
    trimmed and cleaned
salt and pepper

Preheat the barbecue. Cut out 4 squares of double-thickness aluminium foil, each large enough to hold a whole fish.

Reserve 4 basil sprigs for the garnish and chop the remaining basil. Cream the butter in a bowl with a wooden spoon, then beat in the chopped basil and the garlic. Season the fish inside and out with salt and pepper.

Put 1 fish on a piece of foil. Spoon one quarter of the basil and garlic butter into the cavity and wrap the foil around the fish to enclose it completely. Repeat with the remaining fish.

Cook the fish parcels over hot coals for 25–30 minutes, turning once, or until the fish flakes easily when tested with the point of a knife. Transfer the fish parcels to plates and unwrap. Carefully slide out the fish and the cooking juices onto the plates and serve immediately.

Keralan Spiced Fish
in a Parcel

serves 4

4 whole sea bream or small red
    snapper, about 400 g/
    14 oz each
juice of 2 limes
1 tsp sea salt flakes
3 shallots, finely chopped
½ green chilli, deseeded and finely
    chopped
4-cm/1½-inch piece fresh ginger,
    finely chopped
1 tsp black peppercorns, crushed
¼–½ tsp cayenne pepper
1 tsp ground turmeric
vegetable oil for brushing
4 lime wedges, to garnish
thinly sliced red onion, to garnish
plain boiled rice, to serve
pepper

cucumber & radish salsa
2 ridge cucumbers, or 1 long
    cucumber
1 tsp salt
juice of 1 lime
1 garlic clove, finely chopped
2 tbsp chopped fresh mint
4 tbsp diced radishes
¼ tsp sugar

To make the salsa, peel the cucumbers and quarter lengthways. Cut out and discard the seeds, and slice the flesh crossways into small chunks. Put in a sieve placed over a bowl and sprinkle with the salt. Leave to drain for 1 hour, then rinse and pat dry with kitchen paper. Put in a serving bowl and mix with the lime juice, garlic, mint, radishes, sugar, and a little pepper. Cover with clingfilm and set aside.

Preheat the barbecue. Clean and scale the fish, removing the heads. Using a sharp knife, make two diagonal slashes on each side of the fish through the thickest part of the flesh. Put in a shallow dish large enough to take them in a single layer. Combine the lime juice and sea salt, and rub this all over the fish and into the slashes.

Put the shallots, chilli, ginger, peppercorns, cayenne and turmeric into a blender, and whiz to a paste, scraping down the sides of the jar. Smear the paste over the fish, rubbing it in well. Brush four large pieces of kitchen foil with oil. Place a fish on each piece, adding any spice paste left in the dish. Wrap in a loose parcel, sealing well.

Cook the fish over hot coals for 10 minutes. Turn and cook for a further 5 minutes. Place on serving plates and open up the parcels. Garnish with the lime wedges and a few red onion rings. Serve with the salsa and rice.

Halibut Steaks with
Salsa verde

serves 4

2–3 tbsp olive oil
juice of ½ lemon
¼ tsp sea salt flakes
¼ tsp freshly ground black pepper
4 halibut steaks, 2 cm/¾ inch thick,
    about 175 225 g/6–8 oz each
lemon wedges, to serve
warm ciabatta bread, to serve

salsa verde

2 anchovy fillets, rinsed and
    drained
50 g/1¾ oz stale breadcrumbs
25 g/1 oz trimmed flat-leaf parsley
25 g/1 oz fresh basil leaves
2 tbsp capers, rinsed
1 garlic clove, crushed
2 tbsp lemon juice
125 ml/4 fl oz olive oil
salt and pepper

To make the marinade, combine the olive oil, lemon juice, sea salt and pepper in a shallow dish. Add the halibut steaks and turn to coat. Cover with clingfilm and leave to marinate in the refrigerator for 1 hour, turning halfway through. Allow to come to room temperature before cooking.

Preheat the barbecue. Combine all the salsa ingredients in a food processor and briefly pulse 4–5 times to a slightly chunky purée. Pour into a bowl and set aside.

Oil the barbecue rack and a hinged wire grill basket, using a wad of oil-soaked kitchen paper. Place the halibut in the basket, reserving the marinade. Cook over hot coals for 4–6 minutes a side, brushing with the marinade, until golden and the centre of the flesh is opaque when cut into with a small vegetable knife.

Carefully remove the steaks from the basket, and place on warmed serving plates. Serve with lemon wedges, salsa verde and warm ciabatta to mop up the juices.

Orange & Lemon Peppered Monkfish

serves 4

2 oranges
2 lemons
2 monkfish tails, about 500 g/
    1 lb 2 oz each, skinned and
    cut into 4 fillets
8 fresh lemon thyme sprigs
2 tbsp olive oil
2 tbsp green peppercorns, lightly
    crushed
salt

Cut 8 orange slices and 8 lemon slices, reserving the remaining fruit. Rinse the monkfish fillets under cold running water and pat dry with kitchen paper. Place the monkfish fillets, cut side up, on a work surface and divide the citrus slices among them. Top with the lemon thyme. Tie each fillet at intervals with kitchen string to secure the citrus slices and thyme. Place the monkfish in a large, shallow, non-metallic dish.

Squeeze the juice from the remaining fruit and mix with the olive oil in a jug. Season to taste with salt, then spoon the mixture over the fish. Cover with clingfilm and leave to marinate in the refrigerator for up to 1 hour, spooning the marinade over the fish tails once or twice.

Preheat the barbecue. Drain the monkfish tails, reserving the marinade. Sprinkle the crushed green peppercorns over the fish, pressing them in with your fingers. Cook the monkfish over medium–hot coals, turning and brushing frequently with the reserved marinade, for 20–25 minutes. Transfer to a chopping board, remove and discard the string and cut the monkfish tails into slices. Serve immediately.

Monkfish & Prawn Kebabs

serves 4

600 g/1 lb 5 oz monkfish
1 green pepper
1 onion
3 tbsp olive oil
3 tbsp lemon juice
2 garlic cloves, crushed
16 large fresh prawns, peeled and
   deveined
16 fresh bay leaves
salt and pepper

Cut the monkfish into chunks measuring about 2.5 cm/
1 inch. Cut the pepper into similar-sized chunks, discarding
the core and seeds. Cut the onion into 6 wedges then cut
each wedge in half widthways and separate the layers.

To make the marinade, put the oil, lemon juice, garlic, and
salt and pepper to taste in a bowl and whisk together. Add
the monkfish, prawns, onion and pepper pieces and toss
together until coated in the marinade. Cover and leave to
marinate in the fridge for 2–3 hours.

Thread the pieces of fish, prawns, pepper, onion and bay
leaves onto 8 greased, flat metal kebab skewers, alternating
and dividing the ingredients as evenly as possible. Place on a
greased grill pan.

Preheat the barbecue. Cook the kebabs on an oiled rack over
hot coals for 10–15 minutes, turning frequently and basting
with any remaining marinade, until cooked and lightly
charred. Serve hot.

Stuffed
Sardines

serves 6

15 g/½ oz fresh parsley, finely
    chopped
4 garlic cloves, finely chopped
12 fresh sardines, cleaned and
    scaled
3 tbsp lemon juice
85 g/3 oz plain flour
1 tsp ground cumin
salt and pepper
olive oil, for brushing

Place the parsley and garlic in a bowl and mix together.
Rinse the fish inside and out under cold running water and
pat dry with kitchen paper. Spoon the herb mixture into the
fish cavities and pat the remainder all over the outside of the
fish. Sprinkle the sardines with lemon juice and transfer to
a large, shallow, non-metallic dish. Cover with clingfilm and
leave to marinate in the refrigerator for 1 hour.

Preheat the barbecue. Mix the flour and ground cumin
together in a bowl, then season to taste with salt and pepper.
Spread out the seasoned flour on a large plate and gently roll
the sardines in the flour to coat.

Brush the sardines with olive oil and cook over medium–hot
coals for 3–4 minutes on each side. Serve immediately.

Thai Crab Cakes with
Sweet Chilli Sauce

makes 8 cakes

450 g/1 lb cooked white crab meat
6 tbsp chopped fresh coriander
2 eggs, lightly beaten
1 tbsp cornflour
1 tsp Thai fish sauce
1 tsp Thai green curry paste
4 spring onions, finely chopped
1 green chilli, deseeded and finely
   chopped
vegetable oil for brushing
flour for dusting
pepper
sweet chilli sauce (from a bottle),
   to serve
soured cream, to serve

Put the crab meat, coriander, eggs, cornflour, fish sauce and green curry paste in a food processor. Process to a smooth purée. Tip into a bowl, stir in the spring onions and chilli, and season with freshly ground black pepper.

With floured hands, form into 8 patties about 2 cm/¾ inch thick. Place on a greaseproof paper-lined tray and chill for at least 2 hours.

Preheat the barbecue. Oil the barbecue rack and a hinged wire grill basket, using a wad of oil-soaked kitchen paper. Brush the patties with oil on both sides, and arrange in the basket. Cook over medium–hot coals, covered, for 8 minutes until golden. Turn and cook the other side for 4–5 minutes.

Carefully remove the cakes from the basket, using the tip of a small knife to separate them from the wire. Arrange in a warm serving dish, and serve with the chilli sauce and soured cream.

Prawn & Scallop Kebabs

serves 4–6

24 raw tiger prawns, heads
   removed
12 large scallops, corals attached
4–5 tbsp olive oil
juice of 1 lime
1 tbsp chopped fresh coriander
salt and pepper
lime wedges to serve

Preheat the barbecue. Peel the prawns but leave the tails attached. Slit down the back and remove the dark intestinal vein. Remove the tough muscle from the side of the scallops. Slice in half lengthways through the coral.

Combine the olive oil and lime juice in a shallow dish. Add a pinch of salt and pepper. Add the scallops and prawns and leave to marinate for 15 minutes.

Oil the barbecue rack. Reserving the marinade, thread the scallops and prawns alternately onto 8 skewers. Cook over hot coals for 4–6 minutes, turning and brushing with the marinade, until the prawns are pink and cooked through. Arrange on a serving platter, and sprinkle with the coriander and a little more salt and pepper. Serve with lime wedges.

Butterflied Prawns
with Radicchio & Radish Salad

serves 4

16–20 raw tiger prawns with shells
juice of ½ lemon
1 small red chilli, deseeded and finely
　chopped
2 garlic cloves, crushed
3–4 tbsp olive oil
salt and pepper
lemon wedges to serve

salad

3 heads red chicory or 2 small
　radicchio
extra virgin olive oil
squeeze of lemon juice
12 large radishes, trimmed and sliced
　diagonally
½ red onion, thinly sliced into
　crescents
4 tbsp radish sprouts or micro leaves
salt and pepper

Preheat the barbecue. Remove the legs and heads from the prawns, but leave the shell in place. With the backs facing upwards, slice lengthways down the middle, cutting through the shell and not quite through all the flesh. Remove the dark intestinal vein running down the back. Open out the prawns, gently pressing them flat.

Combine the lemon juice, chilli, garlic, olive oil, and salt and pepper in a shallow dish. Add the prawns, turning carefully to coat. Leave to marinate for
15 minutes.

Snap off the chicory leaves and put in a shallow dish. If using radicchio, slice into broad ribbons. Toss with just enough extra virgin olive oil to coat. Sprinkle lightly with lemon juice and salt and pepper. Arrange on a serving platter. Scatter over the radishes, red onion and radish sprouts.

Oil the barbecue rack. Arrange the prawns in a hinged wire grill basket, reserving the marinade. Cook over hot coals, shell-side down, for 1–2 minutes, brushing with the marinade. When the centre of the flesh is still slightly translucent, turn and brush again. Grill the other side for 1 minute or until the flesh is opaque.

Arrange the prawns flesh-side up on top of the salad, garnish with lemon wedges and serve while still warm.

Lobster Halves Topped
with Lemon & Chives

serves 4

2 live lobsters, about 550 g/
  1 lb 4 oz each
75 g/2¾ oz unsalted butter, melted
small bunch of watercress,
  trimmed
juice of ½ lemon
2 tsp snipped chives
salt and pepper
lemon wedges, to serve
crusty bread, to serve

Immediately after purchase, put the lobsters in the freezer at −20°C/−4°F for at least 30 minutes or up to 2 hours. Preheat the barbecue.

Remove the lobsters from the freezer and place on a board. Flatten out the tail and grasp with one hand at the point where the tail joins the body. To kill the lobster instantly, take a wide-bladed pointed knife in the other hand, and plunge it into the centre of the lobster's head, moving the blade towards the eyes. Slice the lobsters in half lengthways through the head, back and tail. Remove and discard the gills, the round whitish stomach sac near the head, and the long intestinal vein running down the side of the tail. The green tomally, or liver, is considered a delicacy. Cut off the claws and lightly crack with a hammer or nutcrackers.

Oil the barbecue rack. Brush the exposed lobster flesh with melted butter, and season with salt and pepper. Place the claws on the rack and cook over hot coals for 2 minutes. Turn and cook for 2 minutes more, leaving them on the grate.

Place the lobster halves on the rack, cut-side down, and cook for 3 minutes. Turn and brush the flesh with melted butter. Cook for 5–10 minutes more, brushing with butter occasionally, or until the flesh becomes white and opaque. Be careful not to overcook.

Arrange the lobster pieces in a warm serving dish with the watercress. Sprinkle with the lemon juice, chives, the remaining melted butter and a little more salt and pepper. Serve with lemon wedges and crusty bread to mop up the juices.

Chargrilled
Devils

serves 6

36 fresh oysters
18 streaky bacon rashers, rinded
1 tbsp mild paprika
1 tsp cayenne pepper

sauce
1 fresh red chilli, deseeded and
    finely chopped
1 garlic clove, finely chopped
1 shallot, finely chopped
2 tbsp finely chopped fresh parsley
2 tbsp lemon juice
salt and pepper

Preheat the barbecue. Open the oysters, catching the juice from the shells in a bowl. Cut the oysters from the bottom shells, reserve and tip any remaining juice into the bowl. To make the sauce, add the red chilli, garlic, shallot, parsley and lemon juice to the bowl, then season to taste with salt and pepper and mix well. Cover the bowl with clingfilm and leave to chill in the refrigerator until required.

Cut each bacon rasher in half across the centre. Season the oysters with paprika and cayenne, then roll each oyster up inside half a bacon rasher. Thread 6 wrapped oysters on to each of the 6 pre-soaked wooden skewers.

Cook over hot coals, turning frequently, for 5 minutes, or until the bacon is well browned and crispy. Transfer to a large serving plate and serve immediately with the sauce.

Grilled Squid with
Chillies & Lemon-garlic Butter

serves 4

6 squid
1–2 red chillies, deseeded and very
    finely chopped
2 tbsp lemon juice
salt and pepper
sunflower oil, for brushing
rocket leaves, to serve
snipped chives, to garnish

lemon-garlic butter
3 large garlic cloves, thinly sliced
55 g/2 oz butter
juice of 2 lemons, strained
sea salt flakes
freshly ground black pepper

Preheat the barbecue. Cut open the squid and spread out the body to make a flat piece. Scrape out the guts and remove the eyes and mouth. Reserve the tentacles. Using a serrated knife, score the inner side of the body with a diamond pattern. Mix the chillies, lemon juice, salt and pepper in a bowl. Add the squid body and tentacles, turning to coat.

To make the lemon-garlic butter, gently fry the garlic in a knob of the butter until just coloured. Add the remaining butter and the lemon juice. Stir until the butter has melted, and season to taste. Pour into a jug and keep warm.

Oil the barbecue rack. Drain the squid, reserving the marinade. Place the tentacles and body, scored-side down, on the grate. Cook over hot coals for 1 minute, then turn, brush with the marinade and cook for 1 minute more until just opaque. Be careful not to overcook.

Arrange a mound of rocket on serving plates. Place the squid on top and sprinkle with chives. Serve with the lemon-garlic butter.

The Vegetable Plot

Portobello
Ciabatta Burgers

serves 4

4 large portobello mushrooms,
   stalks trimmed
2 red peppers, quartered
   lengthways and deseeded
6 tbsp extra virgin olive oil,
   plus extra for brushing
1 large garlic clove, crushed
1 ciabatta loaf
handful of rocket
salt and pepper

Preheat the barbecue. Wipe the mushrooms but do not peel. Put in a dish with the pepper quarters. Whisk together the olive oil and garlic, and pour over the vegetables. Season to taste with salt and pepper.

Slice the ciabatta at a sharp angle into eight 2-cm/¾-inch slices about the same size as the mushrooms. Brush with olive oil.

Oil the barbecue rack. Cook the mushrooms and peppers over medium–hot coals, covered, for 4–5 minutes a side until slightly charred. Remove from the grill and keep warm.

Toast the ciabatta over medium–low coals for 1–2 minutes a side until golden. Place 4 slices on a board and season to taste with salt and pepper. Place a piece of pepper on top, followed by a mushroom and another piece of pepper. Top with a few rocket leaves, season again and finish with the second slice of ciabatta. Serve at once.

Bean Burgers

serves 4

420 g/15 oz canned red kidney
  beans, drained
410 g/14½ oz canned cooked
  chickpeas, drained
1 egg yolk
¼ tsp smoked paprika
50 g/3½ oz fresh breadcrumbs
3 spring onions, finely chopped
oil for brushing
salt and pepper
hamburger buns, soured cream,
  lettuce and sliced tomatoes,
  to serve

Preheat the barbecue to high.

Using a fork, lightly mix the beans, chickpeas, egg yolk, paprika, breadcrumbs, spring onions and salt and pepper to taste, until well combined. Divide the mixture into 4 balls and flatten into patties about 2.5 cm/1 inch thick. Season the outside with salt and pepper, and lightly brush with oil.

Oil the barbecue rack. Cook the burgers for 5 minutes on each side, or until cooked through. Brush the inside of the buns with oil and toast over the barbecue, cut-side down, for 1–2 minutes. Place the burgers in the buns with soured cream, lettuce and tomatoes.

Mushroom Burgers

serves 4

2 tsp sunflower oil, plus extra for
   brushing
115 g/4 oz mushrooms, finely
   chopped
1 carrot, finely chopped
1 onion, finely chopped
1 courgette, finely chopped
25 g/1 oz peanuts
115 g/4 oz fresh white
   breadcrumbs
1 tbsp chopped fresh parsley
1 tsp yeast extract
salt and pepper

Preheat the barbecue to high.

Heat the oil in a heavy-based frying pan, add the mushrooms
and cook, stirring, for 8 minutes, or until all the moisture
has evaporated. Using a slotted spoon, transfer the cooked
mushrooms to a large bowl. Put the carrot, onion, courgette
and peanuts into a food processor and process until finely
chopped. Transfer to the bowl containing the mushrooms
and stir in the breadcrumbs, chopped parsley and yeast
extract. Season to taste with salt and pepper.

Divide the mixture into 4 balls and flatten into patties about
2.5 cm/1 inch thick. Season the outside with salt and pepper.
Place on a large plate, cover with clingfilm and leave to chill
in the refrigerator for at least 1 hour and up to 1 day.

Lightly brush the mushroom burgers with the sunflower oil.
Cook the burgers for 5 minutes on each side, or until cooked
through. Serve immediately.

Halloumi & Red Pepper Sandwiches

makes 4

1 small red pepper, quartered
    lengthways and deseeded
olive oil for brushing
250-g/9-oz block of halloumi
    cheese
small handful fresh oregano leaves,
    shredded
salt and pepper

Preheat the barbecue. Brush the pepper quarters with oil and arrange in a hinged wire grill basket. Cook for 8–10 minutes, turning once, until slightly charred. Remove the skin and slice the flesh crossways into thin strips.

Slice the halloumi horizontally into 8 rectangles, and brush both sides with olive oil. Arrange the sliced pepper and oregano on 4 of the slices. Season with salt and pepper. Make a sandwich with the remaining 4 halloumi slices.

Place the sandwiches in a hinged wire grill basket. Cook over medium–hot coals for 45–60 seconds, turning when the cheese is speckled with brown. Turn and cook the other side for 45 seconds. Serve immediately.

Yakitori vegetable Kebabs

serves 4

1 large courgette, sliced
4 spring onions, sliced diagonally
1 orange pepper, deseeded and
    cubed
100 g/3½ oz button mushrooms,
    wiped clean
8 cherry tomatoes
oil, for brushing
salt and pepper
lime wedges and salad greens,
    to serve

yakitori sauce
1 tbsp soy sauce
1 tbsp clear honey
1 tbsp rice vinegar

Preheat the barbecue to high. Soak the skewers in water for 30 minutes, to prevent burning.

Thread the vegetables alternately onto the wooden skewers and set aside. To make the sauce, mix together all the ingredients and drizzle over the kebabs. Season with salt and pepper and lightly brush the kebabs with oil.

Oil the barbecue rack. Cook the kebabs over medium–hot coals, turning frequently, for 6–10 minutes, or until thoroughly cooked. Transfer to a plate and serve with lime wedges and salad greens.

Marinated Tofu Kebabs

serves 4

2 x 350 g / 12 oz blocks extra firm
   tofu, drained
3 red peppers
12 green salad onions or small
   shallots
24 fresh bay leaves

marinade
2 tbsp Dijon mustard
2 garlic cloves, crushed
2 tbsp sugar
¼ tsp freshly ground black pepper
3 tbsp soy sauce
3 tbsp olive oil

Slice the tofu into 4 x 4 x 2-cm / 1½ x 1½ x ¾-inch cubes.
Combine the marinade ingredients and whisk to a smooth
emulsion. Pour about three-quarters of it into a large shallow
dish and carefully add the tofu in a single layer. Brush the
exposed surfaces with the marinade. Cover with clingfilm
and leave at room temperature for 1–2 hours.

Preheat the barbecue. Slice the peppers lengthways into
quarters, removing the seeds and core. Slice each quarter
crossways into 3.

Trim the onions and slice lengthways in half. Place the
peppers and onions in a dish and brush with the remaining
marinade.

Using 2 thin round metal skewers per kebab, and using
16 in total, carefully thread the tofu onto skewers, alternating
with the onion, peppers and bay leaves. Brush with the
marinade.

Oil the barbecue rack, and place the kebabs on it. Cook over
medium–hot coals for 2–3 minutes, then turn, brush with the
marinade and cook for 2–3 minutes more, or until the tofu is
golden and the vegetables slightly charred.

Vegetable Kebabs
with Blue cheese

serves 4–6

5 thin leeks
250 g/9 oz cremini mushrooms,
    stalks removed
18 small vine-ripened tomatoes,
    halved lengthways
100 g/3½ oz butter, melted
125 g/4½ oz blue cheese,
    crumbled
salt and pepper

Preheat the barbecue to high. Soak the skewers in water for 30 minutes, to prevent burning.

Trim the leeks to about 175 g/6 inches long. Slice in half lengthways, and then crossways into 2.5-cm/1-inch pieces. Thread the leeks, tomatoes and mushrooms alternately onto 12 skewers. Brush with melted butter and season with salt and pepper.

Oil the barbecue rack. Cook the kebabs over medium–hot coals, turning frequently, for 6–10 minutes, or until thoroughly cooked. Transfer to a plate, sprinkle with the cheese whilst still hot and serve.

Rosemary Potatoes

serves 5–6

675 g/1 lb 8 oz medium-sized
   potatoes, unpeeled and
   scrubbed
225 g/8 oz unsalted butter
2 tbsp chopped fresh rosemary
   leaves
salt and pepper

Preheat the barbecue. Slice the potatoes 3 mm/⅛ inch thick.
Plunge into a large bowl of water to wash off the starch.
Drain and blot dry on a tray lined with kitchen paper.

Take a very large sheet of thick foil and smear butter
over an area in the middle measuring about 30 x 20 cm/
12 x 8 inches. Arrange a single layer of potatoes on the
greased area. Sprinkle with some of the rosemary, season
to taste with salt and pepper and dot generously with butter.
Repeat until all the potato slices are used up – there should
be three layers. Fold over the foil to make a flat packet,
sealing and crimping the edges well. Wrap the packet in
2 more large pieces of foil, sealing well.

Cook for 45 minutes over hot coals, turning every
10 minutes, or until the potatoes are tender. Serve straight
from the packet.

Potato Kebabs with Feta

serves 4–6

4 large garlic cloves, peeled
1 tsp sea salt flakes
1 tbsp finely chopped fresh
    rosemary
½ tsp freshly ground black pepper
4 tbsp olive oil
850 g/1 lb 14 oz oval red-skinned
    salad potatoes, about 5 cm/
    2 inches long
40 g/1½ oz crumbled feta cheese
1 tbsp chopped fresh flat-leaf
    parsley

Preheat the barbecue. Using a mortar and pestle, crush the garlic cloves with the sea salt until smooth and creamy. If necessary, push through a sieve to remove any fibrous shreds which could burn. Add the rosemary and pepper, and pound to a paste. Whisk in the olive oil, then pour the mixture into a large bowl and leave to stand.

Scrub the potatoes and slice in half crossways. Steam over boiling water for 7 minutes until only just tender. Spread out on a clean tea towel to dry. Add to the garlic mixture in the bowl and toss to coat.

Arrange the potatoes cut-side down on a board, reserving the remaining garlic mixture in the bowl. Thread onto 6 flat metal skewers, piercing the potato halves through the middle so that the cut sides remain facing downwards.

Heap some of the coals to one side, leaving a slightly cooler zone with a single layer of coals. Oil the barbecue rack. Cook the kebabs over hot coals, cut-side down, for 3–4 minutes, turning when each side is striped from the grill. Brush the upper surface with the garlic oil as you turn. Move to the cooler zone and cook for about 5–7 minutes more, turning and brushing, until tender when pierced with the tip of a knife.

Arrange the kebabs on a serving platter, and sprinkle with the feta and parsley. Serve while still hot.

Glazed Squash
with Walnuts, Mint & Yogurt

serves 4

1 large or 2 small butternut squash
6 tbsp olive oil
2 tbsp aged balsamic vinegar or
  balsamic glaze
1 tsp sea salt flakes, plus extra for
  seasoning
1 tsp freshly ground black pepper
1 handful of walnut halves, toasted
1 small handful of fresh mint leaves
6 tbsp Greek-style yogurt

Preheat the barbecue. Peel and deseed the squash and cut into chunks about 5 cm/2 inches thick. Steam over boiling water for 5–6 minutes or until barely tender. Tip into a large bowl. Whisk together the olive oil, balsamic vinegar, sea salt and freshly ground black pepper. Pour this over the squash, tossing to coat.

Oil the barbecue rack. Drain the squash, reserving the oily juices, and thread onto metal skewers. Cook for 6–7 minutes over medium–hot coals until slightly charred, turning and brushing with the olive oil mixture.

Remove from the skewers and put in a serving bowl. Sprinkle with the toasted walnut halves, mint leaves and a little more sea salt. Drizzle with the yogurt and serve warm or at room temperature.

Baked Sweet Potatoes
with Feta, Coriander Chilli Salsa

serves 4

4 sweet potatoes, about 350 g/
    12 oz each
large knob of butter
2 tbsp chopped fresh coriander
100 g/3½ oz grated feta cheese or
    other hard white cheese
salt and pepper

salsa
3 tomatoes, deseeded and finely
    diced
1 small red onion, finely diced
½ –1 small green chilli, deseeded
    and finely diced
3 tbsp chopped fresh coriander
juice of 1 lime
salt

Preheat the barbecue. Prick the potatoes all over with a fork and wrap in thick foil. Cook over medium–hot coals for 45–55 minutes until easily pierced with a wooden cocktail stick.

Meanwhile, combine the salsa ingredients in a serving bowl. Leave to stand at room temperature to let the flavours develop.

Unwrap the potatoes and remove a thin lengthways slice to expose the flesh. Fork the flesh and mix in a little butter, salt and pepper and most of the coriander. Sprinkle with the cheese and the remaining coriander. Serve with the salsa.

Aubergine &
Mozzarella Sandwiches

serves 4

1 large aubergine
1 tbsp lemon juice
3 tbsp olive oil
salt and pepper
125 g/4½ oz grated mozzarella
   cheese
2 sun-dried tomatoes, chopped

to serve
ciabatta bread
mixed salad leaves
tomato slices

Preheat the barbecue. Using a sharp knife, slice the aubergine into thin rounds.

Mix the lemon juice and olive oil together in a small bowl and season the mixture with salt and pepper to taste. Brush the aubergine slices with the olive oil and lemon juice mixture and cook over medium–hot coals for 2–3 minutes, without turning, until golden on the under side.

Turn half of the aubergine slices over and sprinkle with cheese and chopped sun-dried tomatoes.

Place the remaining aubergine slices on top of the cheese and tomatoes, turning them so that the pale side is uppermost. Barbecue for 1–2 minutes, then carefully turn the whole sandwich over and barbecue for a further 1–2 minutes. Baste with the olive oil mixture.

Serve in ciabatta bread with mixed salad leaves and a few slices of tomato.

Vegetarian Sausages

serves 4

1 tbsp sunflower oil, plus extra for
   oiling
1 small onion, finely chopped
50 g/1¾ oz mushrooms, finely
   chopped
½ red pepper, deseeded and finely
   chopped
400 g/14 oz canned cannellini
   beans, rinsed and drained
100 g/3½ oz fresh breadcrumbs
100 g/3½ oz Cheddar cheese,
   grated
1 tsp dried mixed herbs
1 egg yolk
seasoned plain flour

to serve
small bread rolls
fried onion slices
tomato chutney

Heat the sunflower oil in a saucepan. Add the onion, mushrooms and pepper and fry until softened.

Mash the cannellini beans in a large bowl. Add the onion, mushroom and pepper mixture, the breadcrumbs, cheese, herbs and egg yolk and mix well. Press the mixture together with your fingers and shape into 8 sausages. Roll each sausage in the seasoned flour. Leave to chill in the refrigerator for at least 30 minutes.

Preheat the barbecue. Cook the sausages on a sheet of oiled foil set over medium–hot coals for 15–20 minutes, turning and basting frequently with oil, until golden. Split bread rolls down the centre and insert a layer of fried onions. Place the sausages in the rolls and serve with tomato chutney.

Courgettes on
Grilled Polenta

serves 3–4

2 large yellow or green courgettes
3 tbsp olive oil
1 tsp fresh thyme leaves
coarsely grated zest of ½ lemon
sea salt
tomato salad, to serve

polenta
1 litre/1¾ pints water
½ tsp salt
200 g/7 oz polenta
olive oil, for brushing

To make the polenta, pour the water and salt into a large, heavy-based saucepan. Bring to the boil. Stirring constantly with a long-handled wooden spoon, gradually add the polenta in a thin stream. Stir for 20–30 minutes until the mixture is very smooth and starts to come away from the sides of the pan. Tip into an oiled shallow roasting tray measuring 30 x 20 cm/ 12 x 8 inches. Using a wet palette knife, spread into the corners and level the surface. Once cool and firm, slice into 12 fingers measuring about 10 x 5cm/4 x 2 inches. Remove from the tray and brush both sides with oil.

Preheat the barbecue. Trim the ends from the courgettes. Slice the courgettes lengthways into 1-cm/½-inch thick strips. Carefully peel some of the skin from the outer strips to expose the flesh. Slice the strips in half crossways and place in a shallow dish. Sprinkle with the olive oil, thyme, lemon zest and sea salt, turning to coat. Leave to marinate at room temperature for 30 minutes.

Oil the barbecue rack. Cook the polenta fingers for 5–6 minutes a side, until slightly charred. Remove and keep warm.

Cook the courgette slices over medium–hot coals for 1½–2 minutes, positioning them on the diagonal so they are striped with grill marks. Turn, brush with the marinade, and cook for 1–1½ minutes more until slightly charred. Place the courgettes on the polenta fingers, and serve with a tomato salad.

Avocado-stuffed
Baby Red Peppers

serves 4–6

12 baby red peppers about
    4 cm/1½ inches long, or 4 small
    ordinary peppers
oil for brushing
radish sprouts or micro-leaves,
    to garnish
mixed green salad such as cos
    lettuce, baby spinach and rocket,
    to serve
warm pitta bread fingers
    (see page 190), to serve

avocado stuffing
3 ripe avocados, mashed
juice of 2 limes, or to taste
2 spring onions, including the green
    part, finely chopped
3 tbsp chopped fresh coriander
salt and pepper

Preheat the barbecue. Combine the stuffing ingredients in a bowl. Cover with clingfilm, pressing it over the surface to stop discoloration.

Halve the baby peppers lengthways and scoop out the seeds. (If using ordinary peppers, slice into thirds lengthways, remove the seeds, and cut the thirds in half crossways.) Brush with oil and place in a hinged wire grill basket.

Cook cut-side down over hot coals for 3–4 minutes, or until the edges are slightly charred. Turn and cook for 2–3 minutes more, or until the peppers are just tender but still holding their shape. Remove from the heat and leave to cool. Peel away the skin if it is tough.

Fill each pepper half with a heaped teaspoonful of stuffing. Sprinkle with a few radish sprouts, if using. Arrange on a bed of salad leaves and serve with fingers of warm pitta bread.

Beetroot Parcels

serves 4

8 evenly sized small raw beetroot,
   peeled and quartered lengthways
4 thyme sprigs
olive oil for brushing
salt and pepper
Horseradish Butter (page 18) or
   Tarragon Butter (page 55),
   to serve

Preheat the barbecue. Place 8 beetroot quarters and a thyme sprig on a large square of thick foil. Brush the beetroot with olive oil and sprinkle with salt and pepper. Wrap in a loose parcel, sealing the edges well. Repeat with the remaining beetroot.

Cook the beetroot over medium–hot coals for 30–40 minutes, turning every 10 minutes, until tender. Serve with horseradish butter.

Tomato &
Mozzarella Stacks

serves 4

4 large tomatoes, about
   200 g/7 oz each
225 g/8 oz buffalo mozzarella
24 basil leaves, plus 4 small sprigs
   to garnish
olive oil
salt and pepper

Preheat the barbecue. Using a sharp serrated knife, cut a thin slice from the top and bottom of each tomato, and discard. Slice the rest of the tomato horizontally into three. Slice the mozzarella into thin rounds. Slice the basil leaves into thin ribbons.

Brush the centre of an 18-cm/7-inch square of thick foil with oil. Place a tomato slice on the foil, brush with oil and season to taste with salt and pepper. Add a few basil shreds and a slice of cheese. Continue layering using the second and third tomato slices, seasoning each layer, and finishing with a layer of mozzarella. Fold up the edges of the foil to make a bowl shape. Repeat with the three remaining tomatoes and mozzarella.

Arrange on the grill rack, cook over medium–hot coals, covered, for 8–10 minutes until the top tomato slice is heated through and the mozzarella melted. Garnish with a basil sprig and serve in the foil 'bowls'.

Summer Vegetable Parcels

serves 4

1 kg/2 lb 4 oz mixed baby
  vegetables, such as carrots,
  asparagus, corn cobs, plum
  tomatoes, leeks, courgettes,
  chillies and onions
1 lemon
115 g/4 oz unsalted butter
3 tbsp chopped mixed fresh herbs,
  such as parsley, thyme, chives
  and chervil
2 garlic cloves
salt and pepper

Preheat the barbecue. Cut out 4 x 30-cm/12-inch squares of foil and divide the vegetables equally among them.

Using a grater, finely grate the lemon rind, then squeeze the juice from the lemon and reserve until required. Put the lemon rind, butter, herbs and garlic into a food processor and process until blended, then season to taste with salt and pepper. Alternatively, beat together in a bowl until blended.

Divide the butter equally among the vegetable parcels, dotting it on top. Fold up the sides of the foil to enclose the vegetables, sealing securely. Cook over medium–hot coals, turning occasionally, for 25–30 minutes. Open the parcels, sprinkle with the reserved lemon juice and serve immediately.

Pasta Salad with
Basil vinaigrette

serves 4

225 g/8 oz dried fusilli
4 tomatoes
50 g/1¾ oz black olives
25 g/1 oz sun-dried tomatoes in oil
2 tbsp pine kernels
2 tbsp freshly grated Parmesan
   cheese
salt and pepper
fresh basil leaves, to garnish

vinaigrette
15 g/½ oz basil leaves
1 garlic clove, crushed
2 tbsp freshly grated Parmesan
   cheese
4 tbsp extra virgin olive oil
2 tbsp lemon juice

Cook the pasta in a large saucepan of lightly salted boiling water for 10–12 minutes, or until just tender but still firm to the bite. Drain the pasta, rinse under cold running water, then drain again thoroughly. Place the pasta in a large bowl.

Preheat the barbecue. To make the vinaigrette, place the basil leaves, garlic, cheese, olive oil and lemon juice in a food processor. Season to taste with salt and pepper and process until the leaves are well chopped and the ingredients are combined. Pour the vinaigrette over the pasta and toss to coat.

Cut the tomatoes into wedges. Stone and halve the olives. Slice the sun-dried tomatoes. Place the pine kernels on a baking tray and toast over the barbecue until golden. Add the tomatoes (fresh and sun-dried) and the olives to the pasta and mix until combined. Transfer the pasta to a serving dish, sprinkle over the Parmesan and toasted pine kernels and serve garnished with a few basil leaves.

Italian Vegetable Platter

serves 6

1 large fennel bulb
extra virgin olive oil
1 tsp aged balsamic vinegar or
    balsamic glaze
3 heads chicory
1 large yellow or red pepper
3 large slicing tomatoes
3 green salad onions or 6 spring
    onions
1 garlic clove, finely chopped
sea salt flakes
crushed black peppercorns
chopped flat-leaf parsley to garnish

Preheat the barbecue. Slice a thin sliver from the root end of the fennel bulb, keeping the root intact. Pull off and discard the tough outer layers. Slice the bulb vertically into 8-mm/⅜-inch slices, making sure the layers are still attached to the root. Place in a shallow dish and sprinkle with olive oil, sea salt flakes, crushed peppercorns and the balsamic vinegar. Toss gently to coat.

Trim a thin sliver from the root end of the chicory, discard the outer leaves and slice in half lengthways. Make 2 or 3 lengthways cuts in the core without cutting through to the leaves.

Slice the pepper in half lengthways, and remove the core and seeds. Slice each half lengthways into 3. Slice the tomatoes in half horizontally at their widest point. Trim the salad onions, leaving a good length of stem attached, and slice in half lengthways. If using spring onions, leave them whole.

Oil the barbecue rack. Brush the vegetables with oil and cook over hot coals, starting with the fennel and chicory, adding the remaining vegetables in the order listed. Cook the chicory and tomatoes cut-side down.

After each type of vegetable has cooked for 2 minutes, check the underside. Once slightly charred, turn them over with tongs. Brush the upper surfaces with more oil and sprinkle with sea salt flakes. Sprinkle the tomatoes with the garlic. Cook for another 1–3 minutes, depending on the vegetable.

As the vegetables become cooked, transfer to a warmed serving dish on which they will all fit. Sprinkle with crushed peppercorns and a little more salt, and garnish with chopped parsley. Serve warm or at room temperature.

SideShow

Jacket Potatoes

serves 4

4 large floury potatoes, scrubbed
1 tbsp olive oil
salt

smoked mackerel & soured cream filling
4 smoked peppered mackerel
    fillets, skinned
butter
8 tbsp soured cream
pepper

herby sausage & onion filling
1 tbsp olive oil
1 red onion, finely chopped
8 pork sausages
handful flat-leaf parsley,
    finely chopped
tomato relish or salsa, to serve
pepper

Use some kitchen paper to rub the potatoes with a little olive oil and sprinkle with salt to coat lightly.

Tightly wrap the potatoes in aluminium foil and cook over a barbecue (towards the edge, away from the hottest part), for about 1 hour. The cooking time will depend on the size of potato and the strength of the heat from the fire or barbecue. The potato is ready when it yields to the tip of a sharp knife.

To make the smoked mackerel and soured cream filling, simply flake the smoked mackerel, mash with a little butter and serve on the cooked, opened potato. Drizzle over the soured cream and top with pepper.

To make the herby sausage and onion filling, heat the oil in a non-stick frying pan over the campfire, stove or barbecue and sauté the onion for 5–10 minutes. Squeeze the sausage meat out of its casing and add to the pan. Continue to cook until it is browned and thoroughly cooked, breaking it up with a fork as you go. Stir in the parsley. Serve the sausage meat over the cooked potato with some tomato relish or salsa. Season to taste and serve.

Parsnip & Potato Rosti

serves 6

2 large potatoes
2 parsnips
sunflower oil, for brushing
salt and pepper

Preheat the barbecue. Peel and grate the potatoes and parsnips onto a clean tea towel. Squeeze out any excess liquid, then spread out onto another clean tea towel or kitchen paper and leave to stand for 10 minutes. Put the potatoes and parsnips in a bowl, mix together and season to taste with salt and pepper.

Divide the mixture into 4 balls and flatten into patties about 2.5 cm/1 inch thick. Season the outside with salt and pepper. Place on a large plate, cover with clingfilm and leave to chill in the refrigerator for at least 1 hour and up to 1 day.

Lightly brush the rosti with the sunflower oil and cook for 3–5 minutes on each side, or until cooked through. Serve immediately.

Herby Potato Salad

serves 4–6

butter for greasing
500 g/1 lb 2 oz new potatoes
16 vine-ripened cherry tomatoes,
    halved
70 g/2½ oz black olives, stoned
    and coarsely chopped
4 spring onions, finely sliced
2 tbsp chopped fresh mint
2 tbsp chopped fresh parsley
2 tbsp chopped fresh coriander
juice of 1 lemon
3 tbsp extra virgin olive oil
salt and pepper

Preheat the barbecue. Take a very large sheet of thick foil and smear butter over an area in the middle measuring about 30 x 20 cm/12 x 8 inches. Arrange a single layer of potatoes on the greased area and cook over hot coals for 45 minutes, turning every 10 minutes, or until the potatoes are tender. Once cool, cut into halves or quarters, depending on the size of the potato. Combine with the tomatoes, olives, spring onions and herbs in a bowl.

Mix together the lemon juice and oil in a bowl and pour over the potato salad. Season to taste before serving.

Fresh Potato Salad
with Cornichons & Mustard Vinaigrette

serves 4–6

900 g/2 lb small red-skinned salad
  potatoes, unpeeled
16–18 cornichons, halved
  diagonally
2 tbsp finely chopped red onion
3 tbsp snipped chives
¼ tsp freshly ground black pepper
sea salt flakes, plus extra salt
  for boiling

mustard vinaigrette
2 tsp Dijon mustard
1 tbsp red wine vinegar
¼ tsp freshly ground black pepper
sea salt flakes
4 tbsp extra virgin olive oil

Put the potatoes in a saucepan of water, add salt and bring
to the boil. Reduce the heat to medium and cook for
10–12 minutes until tender. Drain, then return to the pan,
cover with a clean tea towel and leave for a few minutes.

To make the dressing, combine the mustard, vinegar, freshly
ground black pepper and a pinch of sea salt flakes in a
bowl, mixing well. Add the olive oil and whisk until smooth
and thickened.

Put the potatoes in a serving bowl and pour over the
dressing. Add the remaining ingredients and toss gently
to mix. Leave to stand at room temperature for at least
30 minutes before serving.

Corn on the Cob
with Blue cheese

serves 6

140 g/5 oz Danish Blue cheese
140 g/5 oz curd cheese
125 ml/4 fl oz natural Greek yogurt
salt and pepper
6 corn cobs in their husks

Preheat the barbecue. Crumble the Danish Blue cheese, then place in a bowl. Beat with a wooden spoon until creamy. Beat in the curd cheese until thoroughly blended. Gradually beat in the yogurt and season to taste with salt and pepper. Cover with clingfilm and leave to chill somewhere cool until required.

Fold back the husks on each corn cob and remove the silks. Smooth the husks back into place. Cut out 6 rectangles of double-thickness aluminium foil, each large enough to enclose a corn cob. Wrap the corn cobs in the foil.

Cook the corn cobs over the barbecue for 15–20 minutes, turning frequently. Unwrap the corn cobs and discard the foil. Peel back the husk on one side of each and trim off with a sharp knife. Serve with the blue cheese dressing.

Baked Camembert

serves 4

1 whole Camembert
   (about 200 g/7 oz)
2 cloves garlic, thinly sliced
2 sprigs rosemary, cut into small
   pieces
4 tbsp white wine (optional)
salt and pepper
crusty French bread, to serve

Preheat the barbecue. Remove the Camembert from its wrapper and place on a piece of double-thickness aluminium foil.

Make about 8–10 small incisions in the surface of the cheese using the tip of a small sharp knife.

Push the garlic slices and rosemary sprigs into the incisions and then drizzle over the wine (if using.) Add a little seasoning.

Loosely seal the foil and then cook directly on the edge of the barbecue for about 10–15 minutes, depending on the heat levels, until the cheese has become soft and molten in the centre.

Serve with crusty French bread.

Three-cheese Dip
with Grilled Pitta Bread

serves 4

150 g/5½ oz cream cheese
75 g/2¾ oz feta cheese, crumbled
40 g/1½ oz Cheddar cheese,
    coarsely grated
3 tbsp snipped chives
1 tsp coarsely grated lemon zest
4 pitta breads
olive oil for brushing
salt and pepper

Preheat the barbecue. Combine the three cheeses in a bowl, mixing lightly with a fork. Stir in the chives and lemon zest, and season to taste with salt and pepper.

Open out the pitta breads to make 8 halves. Slice each half crossways to make 16 pieces. Brush the cut surfaces with olive oil, and sprinkle with a little salt and pepper.

Oil the barbecue rack. Grill the pitta bread over medium–hot coals, cut-side down, for 45–60 seconds a side, or until golden. Serve with the cheese dip.

Garlic Bread

serves 6

150 g/5½ oz butter, softened
3 cloves garlic, crushed
2 tbsp chopped parsley
pepper
1 large or 2 small sticks
     of French bread

Preheat the barbecue. Mix together the butter, garlic and parsley in a bowl until well combined. Season with pepper to taste and mix well.

Make several lengthways cuts in the bread but be careful not to cut all the way through.

Spread the flavoured butter over one side of each cut and place the loaf on a large sheet of aluminium foil.

Wrap the bread in aluminium foil and cook over hot coals for 10–15 minutes, until the butter melts and the bread is piping hot.

Bruschetta with
Roasted Aubergine Purée

makes about 24

2 small aubergines
1 tbsp extra virgin olive oil, plus
    extra for brushing
1 large garlic clove, crushed
juice of ½ lemon
¼ tsp cumin seeds, crushed
pinch cayenne
¼ tsp sea salt flakes
¼ tsp freshly ground black pepper
2 tbsp chopped fresh flat-leaf
    parsley
1 ciabatta loaf, thickly sliced at an
    angle

Preheat the barbecue. Prick the aubergines all over with a fork. Oil the barbecue rack. Cook over medium–hot coals for 15 minutes, turning every 5 minutes, until very charred on the outside and soft in the centre. Remove from the heat and leave until cool enough to handle.

Remove the charred skin from the aubergines and drain the flesh briefly to get rid of excess liquid. Put in a food processor with the tablespoon of olive oil, the garlic, lemon juice, cumin, cayenne, salt and pepper. Whiz to a purée, and tip into a serving bowl. Stir in the parsley, and check the seasoning. Add more salt, pepper and lemon juice if necessary.

Brush the ciabatta slices on both sides with olive oil. Toast over medium coals for 1–2 minutes a side until golden. Remove from the grill. Spread a thick layer of aubergine purée over each slice, then cut in half. Serve while still warm or at room temperature.

Roasted Balsamic &
Honey onions

serves 4

4 red onions, peeled and cut into
  chunky wedges
4 tsp clear honey
4 tbsp balsamic vinegar
1 tsp fresh thyme,
  finely chopped
salt and pepper

Divide the onion wedges between 4 squares of double-thickness aluminium foil. Bring up the sides of the foil a little.

Drizzle the honey and balsamic vinegar over the onions, add the thyme and season.

Loosely seal the parcels and cook over hot coals for 15–20 minutes until the onions are tender.

Crispy Bacon &
Spinach Salad

serves 4

4 tbsp olive oil
4 rashers of streaky bacon, diced
1 thick slice of white bread,
    crusts removed, cut into cubes
450 g/1 lb fresh spinach,
    torn or shredded

Heat 2 tablespoons of the oil in a large non-stick frying pan over a barbecue. Add the diced bacon to the pan and cook for 3–4 minutes, or until crisp. Remove with a slotted spoon, draining carefully, and set aside.

Toss the cubes of bread in the fat remaining in the pan over the heat for about 4 minutes, or until crisp and golden. Remove the croûtons with a slotted spoon, draining carefully, and set them aside.

Add the remaining oil to the frying pan and heat. Toss the spinach in the oil over a high heat for about 3 minutes, or until it has just wilted. Turn into a serving bowl and sprinkle with the bacon and croûtons. Serve immediately.

Grilled Pineapple with Mint

serves 4–6

1 ripe pineapple
60 g/2¼ oz unsalted butter, melted
4 tbsp Demerara sugar
2 tbsp chopped fresh mint

Preheat the barbecue. Peel the pineapple and slice horizontally into 2-cm/¾-inch rings. Cut the rings in half to make semi-circles and remove the core. Mix the melted butter and 2 tablespoons of the sugar in a shallow dish. Add the pineapple, turning to coat and taking care not to break the semi-circles.

Using a mortar and pestle, grind the mint with the remaining sugar, and set aside.

Arrange the pineapple in a hinged wire grill basket, reserving the buttery juices. Cook for 2–3 minutes over medium–hot coals, brushing with the juices. Turn and cook for 2–3 minutes more, brushing, until slightly charred.

Arrange in a warm dish, sprinkle with the ground sugar and mint, and serve while still warm.

Caramelized Apple Rings

serves 4

4 crisp apples, such as Braeburn
juice of ½ lemon
3 tbsp Demerara sugar
¼ tsp ground cinnamon
25 g/1 oz melted butter
vanilla ice cream or clotted cream,
    to serve

Preheat the barbecue. Remove and discard a thin slice from the top and bottom of the apples. Remove the cores and slice each apple into 3 thick rings. Put in a bowl and toss with the lemon juice to prevent discoloration.

Mix the sugar and cinnamon, and sprinkle over the apples, tossing thoroughly to coat. Brush with melted butter on both sides, and place in a greased hinged wire grill basket, reserving the liquid in the bowl.

Cook for 5–6 minutes over hot coals until golden and slightly charred, turning every 2 minutes and brushing with butter and the reserved liquid. Serve with vanilla ice cream or clotted cream.

Nectarine
Parcels

serves 4

8 ripe nectarines
50 g/1¾ oz unsalted butter, plus
    extra for greasing
3 tbsp Demerara sugar
Amaretti liqueur or cognac
    (optional)
vanilla ice cream to serve

Preheat the barbecue. Take eight 20-cm/8-inch squares of thick aluminium foil and grease the centre of each with butter. Place a nectarine on each square of foil. Top with a small knob of butter, a sprinkle of sugar, and a few drops of liqueur, if using. Wrap the foil into a loose parcel, sealing well.

Cook over medium–low coals, covered, for 15–20 minutes until tender when pierced with a wooden cocktail stick. Serve warm with the ice cream.

Banana & Dark Chocolate S'mores

serves 4

8 marshmallows
8 chocolate chip cookies
1 banana, thinly sliced
4 squares dark chocolate

Preheat the barbecue. If using wooden kebab skewers, soak 1 per person in cold water for 30 minutes first to prevent burning.

Thread the marshmallows, 2 at a time, onto the pre-soaked wooden skewers or metal skewers and toast over the barbecue until they soften.

Place the soft marshmallows onto 1 cookie, top with a few slices of banana and a square of chocolate, and sandwich together with the other cookie. Repeat with the remaining biscuits and marshmallows.

Chocolate & Rum Bananas

serves 4

1 tbsp butter
225 g/8 oz plain or milk chocolate
4 large bananas
2 tbsp rum
mascarpone cheese, to serve

Preheat the barbecue. Take four large squares of double-thickness aluminium foil and brush them with butter.

Cut the chocolate into very small pieces. Carefully make a slit, lengthways, in the peel of each banana, and open just wide enough to insert the chocolate. Place the chocolate pieces inside the bananas, along their lengths, then close them up.

Wrap each stuffed banana in a square of foil and cook over the barbecue for 5–10 minutes, or until the chocolate has melted inside the bananas. Remove from the heat, place the bananas on plates and pour some rum into each banana.

Serve with mascarpone cheese for a messy but truly indulgent treat.

Fruit Skewers

serves 4

a selection of fruit, such as
    apricots, peaches, strawberries,
    mangoes, pineapple, bananas,
    prepared and cut into chunks
maple syrup
50 g/1¾ oz plain chocolate, broken
    into chunks

Preheat the barbecue. If using wooden kebab skewers, soak 1 per person in cold water for 30 minutes first to prevent burning.

Thread alternate pieces of fruit onto the pre-soaked wooden skewers or metal skewers. Brush the fruit with a little maple syrup.

Put the chocolate in a heatproof bowl, set the bowl over a saucepan of barely simmering water and heat over the barbecue, until the chocolate has melted.

Meanwhile, cook the skewers over the barbecue for 3 minutes, or until caramelized. Serve drizzled with a little of the melted chocolate.

Mojito

serves 1

1 tsp syrup de gomme
a few fresh mint leaves
juice of ½ lime
ice cubes
2 measures Jamaican rum
soda water, to top up
dash Angostura bitters

Put the syrup, mint leaves and lime juice in a highball glass and crush or muddle the mint leaves.

Add ice and rum, then top up with soda water to taste.

Finish with a dash of Angostura bitters.

Orange & Lime Iced Tea

serves 2

300 ml/10 fl oz water
2 tea bags
100 ml/3½ fl oz orange juice
4 tbsp lime juice
1–2 tbsp brown sugar
8 ice cubes

to decorate
wedge of lime
granulated sugar
slices of fresh orange, lemon
   or lime

Pour the water into a saucepan and bring to the boil. Remove from the heat, add the tea bags and leave to infuse for 5 minutes. Remove the tea bags and leave the tea to cool to room temperature (about 30 minutes). Transfer to a jug, cover with clingfilm and chill in the refrigerator for at least 45 minutes.

When the tea has chilled, pour in the orange juice and lime juice. Add sugar to taste.

Take two glasses and rub the rims with a wedge of lime, then dip them in granulated sugar to frost. Put the ice cubes into the glasses and pour over the tea. Decorate with slices of fresh orange, lemon or lime and serve.

Singapore Sling

serves 1

10–12 cracked ice cubes
2 measures gin
1 measure cherry brandy
1 measure lemon juice
1 tsp grenadine
soda water, to top up

to decorate
lime peel
cocktail cherries

Put 4–6 cracked ice cubes into a cocktail shaker. Pour the gin, cherry brandy, lemon juice and grenadine over the ice. Shake vigorously until a frost forms.

Half fill a chilled highball glass with cracked ice cubes and strain the cocktail over them. Top up with soda water and decorate with lime peel and cocktail cherries.

Margarita

serves 1

lime wedge
coarse salt
4–6 cracked ice cubes
3 measures white tequila
1 measure triple sec
2 measures lime juice
slice of lime, to decorate

Rub the rim of a chilled cocktail glass with the lime wedge and then dip in a saucer of coarse salt to frost.

Put the cracked ice cubes into a cocktail shaker. Pour the tequila, triple sec and lime juice over the ice. Shake vigorously until a frost forms.

Strain into the prepared glass and decorate with the lime slice.